THE MULTILATERAL DEVELOPMENT BANKS
Improving U.S. Leadership

THE WASHINGTON PAPERS

. . . intended to meet the need for an authoritative, yet prompt, public appraisal of the major developments in world affairs.

Series Editor: Walter Laqueur

Managing Editor: Donna R. Spitler

MANUSCRIPT SUBMISSION

The Washington Papers and Praeger Publishers welcome inquiries concerning manuscript submissions. Please include with your inquiry a curriculum vitae, synopsis, table of contents, and estimated manuscript length. Manuscript length must fall between 30,000 and 45,000 words. All submissions will be peer reviewed. Submissions to *The Washington Papers* should be sent to *The Washington Papers*; The Center for Strategic and International Studies; 1800 K Street NW; Suite 400; Washington, DC 20006. Book proposals should be sent to Praeger Publishers; 88 Post Road West; P.O. Box 5007; Westport, CT 06881-5007.

THE WASHINGTON PAPERS/178

THE MULTILATERAL DEVELOPMENT BANKS

Improving U.S. Leadership

Barbara Upton

Foreword by Sidney Weintraub

Published with the Center for Strategic
and International Studies, Washington, D.C.

PRAEGER

Westport, Connecticut
London

Library of Congress Cataloging-in-Publication Data

Upton, Barbara.
The multilateral development banks : improving U.S. leadership/
Barbara Upton.
p.cm. — (The Washington papers ; 178)
"Published with the Center for Strategic and International
Studies, Washington, D.C."
Includes bibliographical references and index.
ISBN 0-275-96966-5 (cloth) — ISBN 0-275-96967-3 (paper)
1. Development banks—United States—Management. I. Title. II. Series.
HG1976.U6 U67 2000
332.1'53—dc21 99-057875

The Washington Papers are written under the auspices of the Center for Strategic and International Studies (CSIS) and published with CSIS by Praeger Publishers. CSIS, as a public policy research institution, does not take specific policy positions. Accordingly, all views, positions, and conclusions expressed in the volumes of this series should be understood to be solely those of the authors.

British Library Cataloguing-in-Publication Data is available.

Library of Congress Catalog Card Number: 99-057875
ISBN: 0-275-96966-5 (cloth)
0-275-96967-3 (paper)

First published in 2000

Praeger Publishers, 88 Post Road West, Westport, CT 06881
An imprint of Greenwood Publishing Group, Inc.

Printed in the United States of America

The paper used in this book complies with the Permanent
Paper Standard issued by the National Information Standards
Organization (Z39.48-1984).

10 9 8 7 6 5 4 3 2 1

Contents

Foreword

The establishment of the World Bank after World War II was a significant act of economic statesmanship. Whatever one's opinion about its proper role in the future, there can be little legitimate dissent to the fact that the Bank contributed significantly to world development in the decades after its birth.

The Bank's role has changed over the years. The creation of the World Bank—more precisely, the International Bank for Reconstruction and Development (IBRD)—came at a time when global financing, particularly for the reconstruction of Europe (the "R" in the IBRD title), was largely nonexistent. The IBRD provided a mechanism to attract this financing by drawing on an implicit guarantee of repayment from the Bank's collective members. The IBRD borrows on world money markets, using the assurance of what is known as the "callable capital" of the member countries, and then on-lends for projects and programs in the individual countries. In addition to making capital available, the Bank provided expertise to shape and evaluate projects. It still does. The callable capital literally can be called in the event of borrowing country defaults, but this action has never been necessary.

As reconstruction in the developed countries was completed, the IBRD shifted its emphasis to developing countries. The developed countries by then could raise needed capital on their own, but the IBRD served as an intermediary between the money markets and the developing country borrowers because it could obtain funds at the interest rate of a premier borrower, whereas most developing countries could not. Because the source of the money was the private capital market, the on-lending by the IBRD could not be at a concessional rate. This nonconcessional interest rate was suitable for the more economically advanced developing countries, but not for the abysmally poor ones. Consequently, a separate lending window was created, the International Development Association (IDA), from which loans to the poorest developing countries were made on terms of up to 40 years, a 10-year grace period before any repayments were required, and an annual interest charge of less than 1 percent—in other words, more grant than loan. The Bank cannot obtain resources for these near grants from private markets, and member governments therefore must make direct appropriations to fund IDA.

The Bank further evolved and added another affiliate, the International Finance Corporation (IFC), which lends to private corporations, usually together with other investors. In due course, another affiliate was added, the Multilateral Investment Guarantee Agency (MIGA). The World Bank Group is the shorthand term for these collective affiliated bodies.

The multilateral development assistance structure grew beyond this worldwide institution, and a number of regional development banks were later created—the Inter-American Development Bank (IDB), the Asian Development Bank, the African Development Bank, and, most recently, the European Bank for Reconstruction and Development. These banks have regular windows (akin to the IBRD window in the World Bank) and may also have soft loan windows (similar to IDA), and for the IDB, a private sector affiliate comparable to the IFC exists. The World Bank remains the largest of the development banks; its commitments and actual disbursements are greater than all the others combined. Barbara Upton describes the structure of these multilateral development banks (MDBs) in some detail in the pages that follow.

Their structure is complex. The development banks are both global and regional, and the provision of loans is both concessional and near-commercial. Each geographic region takes pride in its development bank, and the principle of subsidiarity prevails—that is, the conviction that the best institution is one closest to the people.

More than 50 years have passed since the original creation of the IBRD, and the situation that existed at the outset—the unavailability of global credit from private markets—no longer applies. Indeed, private capital movements now dwarf those from the MDBs. The data are provided in this volume. In 1997, all flows from the MDBs amounted to $28 billion, of which $17 billion were concessional and $11 billion nonconcessional. By contrast, private capital flows from developed to developing countries in 1997 were $252 billion, nine times larger, and of that, direct foreign investment was $107 billion. Direct investment flows are reasonably comparable to disbursements from the MDBs in that they too are intended to bring returns over the long term.

There are limits, however, to exclusive reliance on private capital flows. Athough much infrastructure—roads, ports, sewage systems, water and irrigation facilities, and the like—can be financed from private sources, a good deal cannot. Financing the public education structure—kindergarten through grade 12 and state institutions of higher education—is essentially the responsibility of the state at various levels. Financing of health delivery systems—hospitals, clinics, laboratories—is predominantly a public responsibility in developing countries.

In addition, the large figure for capital flows to developing countries masks the uneven distribution of these funds. The more economically advanced developing countries can be attractive places for private foreign investment, whereas the poorest countries receive little of these flows. The MDBs, therefore, still have a large role to play in the world's poorest countries. The domestic generation of investment capital, either by the public or private sector, is by definition inadequate in these countries—else they would not be so desperately poor.

The president of the World Bank, James Wolfensohn, makes these points repeatedly in his public statements. His primary focus is to reduce the unconscionably high level of poverty in developing countries. This philosophic emphasis leads to the conclusion that the key role of the MDBs is to concentrate its efforts in those countries where private capital flows cannot meet the pressing needs. This is mainly in the world's poorest countries, but not exclusively, because poverty is substantial in many intermediate developing countries. The figures given above showing that the concessional funds from the MDBs are larger than the nonconcessional flows demonstrate that this priority does prevail in actual operations.

The MDBs are not the only providers of development assistance. Barbara Upton's data show that bilateral concessional aid flows were close to double those from the MDBs in 1997. Her central analysis focuses on how the United States government makes its decisions in dealing with the MDBs and how its procedures can be improved. The proverbial alien from Mars, if landing in Washington, D.C., would logically expect meticulous coordination to occur between the two programs, multilateral and bilateral. The source of funds is the same when it comes to concessional transfers—namely, the U.S. taxpayer. Barbara Upton concludes that the coordination is spotty—and that is a kind word. The Agency for International Development handles the bilateral program and the Treasury Department is responsible for U.S. participation in the MDBs—and each is jealous of its turf.

Beyond that, U.S. official development assistance (that is, concessional aid flows) was only 0.09 percent (less than one-tenth of 1 percent) of U.S. gross domestic product in 1997. The United States stands last among all donor countries of the Development Assistance Committee of the Organization for Economic Cooperation and Development in this respect. As U.S. bilateral aid has declined, U.S. participation in the MDBs has become relatively more important.

The American public is generally uninformed about U.S. development assistance, whether provided directly or through MDBs. Polls show that the public believes that the level of U.S. aid is many multiples of what it actually is. The public, however, is aware of the growing poverty in developing countries—it is shown regularly on television screens—and considers the United States to be a generous and compassionate nation. Is this compassion given adequate attention in the formulation of U.S. foreign policy? It would seem not from the relatively low level of U.S. development assistance. It is in this context that this book on the effectiveness of U.S. participation in the MDBs should be read. Barbara Upton reaches the conclusion that we can and should do better.

Sidney Weintraub
January 2000

Preface

This volume constitutes the second and final part of the project on the United States and the multilateral development banks (MDBs) undertaken by the Center for Strategic and International Studies. The first part was an 18-month task force on the role and future directions of the MDBs from the U.S. perspective. The task force was cochaired by Senator Bill Bradley and Congressman John Kasich, and its final report was published in March 1998. The task force report included a number of conclusions about desirable future directions for the MDBs and recommendations about themes and, in some cases, specific positions the United States should advocate in its interactions with the institutions and their other members.

This study examines the process by which the United States formulates and implements its policies toward the multilateral banks and related programs to determine whether it is adequate to generate the kind of decisive, thoughtful, and constructive U.S. leadership that is required. In preparing this study, I am indebted to the many individuals who generously gave their time in interviews, both on and off the record, who provided comments on early drafts, and who responded to extensive follow-up questions at various stages.

The project was supported by grants from the Ford Foundation and 18 U.S. corporations.

Barbara Upton
Director
United States and the MDBs Project

Introduction

The United States and Multilateral Institutions— A Widening Disconnect

The end of the Cold War was supposed to usher in a new era of cooperative international problem solving. Many believed its hallmark would be the growing prominence of multilateral institutions, especially in areas of rapidly increasing international interdependence such as economics, trade, and finance. Instead, as the new millennium begins, many Americans seem to distrust multilateral institutions, and some of the most prominent institutions are facing stronger criticism than ever.

The United Nations is widely viewed as ineffective and, by some, as desiring to encroach on U.S. sovereignty. The multilateral trading system and its oversight entity, the World Trade Organization (WTO), are viewed by many as harmful to U.S. workers and likely to lead to declines in U.S. environmental standards. The International Monetary Fund (IMF), enmeshed in difficult rescue operations and reeling from costly failure in Russia, faces unprecedented challenge to its economic prescriptions from mainstream economists. It also faces heightened criticism for its secretive operating style and willingness to participate in programs that some believe allow international creditors to avoid paying a fair penalty for misjudgments.

Meanwhile, the five multilateral development banks (MDBs) ponder their future as potentially available private resources outstrip their programs by larger amounts and as some countries they have touted as their greatest successes struggle to recover from economic collapse. Often the structural weaknesses in developing economies revealed by the 1997–1998 economic crisis have come in such areas as the financial sector, where the MDBs have been large lenders for decades, thus raising questions about the institutions' effectiveness in securing meaningful reforms. At the same time, many of the civic groups most supportive of international development regard the MDBs with skepticism, and some continue to proclaim that "fifty years is enough."[1]

In a concrete manifestation of U.S. ambivalence about, and in a number of quarters dislike of, multilateral institutions, the administration and Congress (under both parties) have failed to reach agreement on the role the United States sees for various multilateral institutions and the desirable scope of U.S. participation in them. As a result, Congress has persistently failed to appropriate funding in a timely manner to meet commitments that various administrations have negotiated. Congress has also specified very detailed conditions for continued U.S. funding of specific institutions—conditions that it says should be presented to the institution and its other members on a "take it or leave it basis."

Not only are specific international organizations unpopular with large segments of the American public and their representatives in Congress, but the concept of multilateralism appears to have little political legitimacy among many groups in American society.

In addition to a lack of support from their most powerful shareholder, many of the multilateral economic institutions born after World War II or developed during the Cold War have encountered other problems. In the past several years a number of studies conducted by these institutions and their supporters have sharply criticized their management practices and ability to define and accomplish objectives.

The government of Denmark, long one of the strongest supporters of multilateral approaches, noted in its 1996 *Plan of Action for Active Multilateralism:*

> The rationalization measures which characterize both the public and private sectors in donor and recipient countries all over the world do not yet appear to have penetrated international organizations to any marked degree. On a number of occasions, particularly in some of the organizations within the UN system, and up until recently in the African Development Bank, we have seen management without vision, conviction or authority, and irresponsible or aimless administration including in matters of accounting.[2]

World Bank president James Wolfensohn's 1997 *Strategic Compact*, aimed at improving the effectiveness of that institution, states that

> • Close to one third of Bank-supported projects have unsatisfactory outcomes. . . .
> • There is a lack of professional expertise in key areas . . . and
> • Clients complain about the Bank's slowness and standardized approach, while many potential partners have become critics.[3]

Drawing on internal documents, the *Financial Times* recently featured reports that the United Nations High Commissioner for Refugees (UNHCR), often considered one of the best UN agencies, is "wasting millions of dollars donated by western governments because of incompetent management, dubious accounting practices, and alleged fraud."[4]

Finally, two former U.S. secretaries of the Treasury, George Shultz and William Simon, charged with managing U.S. policy toward the IMF in earlier days, recently called for its abolition on the grounds it now is "ineffective, unnecessary, and obsolete."[5]

The performance problems of some multilateral institutions and their unpopularity in the United States are mutually reinforcing. Doubts about the institutions' value on the part of their most powerful shareholder reinforce uncertainty and drift in the organizations themselves. These uncertainties in turn reduce the institutions' effectiveness, which leads to more skepticism about their value.

This volume explores whether an important cause of the growing disconnect between Americans and multilateral institutions, and of some of their recent performance problems, lies in how the United States manages its participation in them.

By pushing unrealistic or contradictory mandates upon multilateral institutions, aggressively seeking the appointment of inappropriate individuals to leadership positions, and failing to deal, in some cases for decades, with obvious problems, the United States may have played an important role in the poor performance of many multilateral institutions and then sought to blame the institutions for the ensuing failures.[6] These weaknesses in U.S. policies toward multilateral institutions may be rooted in outdated U.S. government structures and processes that compartmentalize multifaceted problems and fail to bring to bear the best available expertise. These outdated processes also fail to produce meaningful dialogue among all decisionmakers or timely decisions among alternatives.

This study does not begin from the presumption that multilateral institutions are necessarily either helpful or harmful to U.S. interests. Given the multicountry implications of many problems and the porous nature of national borders, the United States will likely need to address a number of issues through international institutions of various kinds. When it does so, the United States will need them to function effectively and be able to secure enough support from the Congress, the public, and other members to garner adequate resources.

U.S. management of its role in multilateral institutions is important because adrift and floundering institutions can cause the United States considerable trouble by advancing irresponsible proposals on important issues. As former secretary of state and of the Treasury George Shultz has noted: "Organizations with no clear mandate and scads of money are dangerous."[7] The United States should thus have a policy process that enables it to play a constructive leadership role in needed multilateral institutions and that takes decisive action to remedy problems in poorly performing organizations or ones whose functions have lost relevance.

The U.S. stance in multilateral institutions is especially important because it is difficult for many institutions to function well without effective U.S. leadership, to some degree because of elements built into their structures at inception. The United States is one of five nations wielding a veto in the United Nations (UN) Security Council and the only member with the voting power to veto changes in the governing charters of a number of institutions. The United States also has the informal right to nominate the president of the World Bank, the second ranking official at the IMF, and senior officials at three of the four regional development banks. Three of the five heads of major UN funds and programs were nominated by the United States.

The United States occupies a special place in most multilateral institutions because of its economic size and strength and its role as the only military superpower. For various reasons, other nations that have attributes needed for leadership in multilateral institutions have not chosen to strongly assert such a role—Germany and Japan for historical reasons and Russia because of economic weakness. The European Union has been hampered by continuing internal divisions and the need to focus on its own future evolution.

The United States needs an effective and persuasive U.S. policy toward multilateral institutions because current divisions—between the executive branch and Congress and among the various factions of each—have become so troublesome to other members of multilateral institutions that they have become irritants in U.S. bilateral relations with important allies. Likewise, serious problems with the content or style of U.S. management of its role in these institutions can affect foreign leaders' perceptions on other issues.[8]

This volume examines the U.S. policy process toward the five multilateral development banks—the World Bank Group, the Inter-American Development Bank, the Asian Development Bank, the African Development Bank, and the European Bank for Reconstruction and Development—as a case study in how the United States manages its participation in multilateral institutions. The management of the U.S. role in these institutions is reviewed because these institutions are playing an increasingly important role in the official U.S. relationship with the developing world and because, for the most part, they are examples of mature institutions being called upon to adapt their roles and operating styles to new financial and political realities. U.S. policymaking toward the MDBs does not face the harsh polarization that it does in the case of the United Nations, but it does face numerous serious challenges. How the United States deals with these challenges will affect U.S. relations with developed and developing countries alike.

Chapter 1 examines the evolving role of the MDBs from the U.S. perspective. Chapter 2 describes the U.S. policy process toward the banks, and chapter 3 offers conclusions on its strengths and weaknesses. Chapter 4 contains recommendations for improving the process, and chapter 5 looks at the broader, more general lessons for U.S. policy formulation on multilateral institutions.

1

The United States and the Multilateral Development Banks

At the Outset: A Clear and Simple Mandate

The multilateral development banks (MDBs) were established, in most cases at the instigation of the United States, as innovative financial vehicles to provide loans to countries and projects where the funds would have a high economic rate of return, but where perceived risk would preclude private financing. The governments of member nations own the MDBs and funded their initial expenditures directly with the convertible currency subscriptions of the wealthier members. The institutions' unique financial advantage is provided by their "callable capital" feature. Each country's capital subscription is divided into two parts. The first or "paid-in" portion can be used to finance expenditures directly. However, the second and larger part of the subscription—callable capital—is never actually transferred to the institution but is regarded as legally available and is used to guarantee the bank's borrowings on international capital markets. In this way wealthy countries are able to make available much more money to the institution than they are required to pay out from their own budgets, unless the institution cannot repay its borrowings and must make a "call" on its callable capital—a situation that has never occurred.

This mechanism for financing the MDBs was established when the World Bank was created at the Bretton Woods conference near the end of World War II. Although the first borrowers from the

World Bank were war-ravaged European countries and Japan, the bulk of funding soon was directed toward the larger, wealthier developing countries that could afford the institution's credit terms—which had to be hard enough to cover the bank's cost of borrowing most of its funds on the international bond market. The MDB system was expanded to provide more funding to the wealthier Latin American countries with the creation of the Inter-American Development Bank (IDB) in 1959, headquartered, like the World Bank, in Washington, D.C.

The financial leverage feature of these institutions proved to work very well. Loans were extended for a wide variety of purposes but especially for the construction of such infrastructure as power plants, roads, and potable water systems. In almost all cases, the recipient government guaranteed the loans, protecting the MDB from arrears or default if the project did not prove financially viable. As the multilateral banks gained a cushion of financial reserves, diversified their risks across countries and sectors, and enjoyed nearly perfect repayment rates, it became possible for the wealthier members to finance new funding increments or "replenishments" largely by callable capital. By the 1990s about 98 percent of new capital was being provided to the older multilateral banks in callable capital form.

An Expanding Mandate

As the Cold War intensified, the MDBs came to be seen as one of the free world's tools for combating communism. Both the size and the country coverage of MDB lending were extended, as were the types of projects for which the institutions provided funding. The Asian Development Bank (ADB), based in Manila, was established in 1966 as the U.S. military buildup in Vietnam accelerated.

In the 1950s it became clear that the callable capital funding mechanism that enabled the MDBs to transfer significant resources to developing countries at low cost to the donors precluded the institutions from lending much to the large group of countries that could not repay loans made at near-market interest rates. These countries were not victims of a capital market imperfection, as it was often said the richer borrowers were. No amount of better information or ability to spread risk would enable countries such as Honduras, Bolivia, Bangladesh, or most Sub-Saharan African countries to repay loans on terms that would cover the costs of capital on international bond markets.

Therefore, the MDBs formed companion institutions or separate lending "windows" that operated on a completely different financial basis. These windows lent to the poorer countries convertible currency donations from wealthier members plus funds provided by repayments of principal and interest from previous loans. Loan repayments built up slowly at first because these MDB "soft loan windows" generally lent for 40 years with a 10-year grace period, with interest at only 1 to 2 percent per year.

With the creation of these soft loan affiliates or windows the intellectual rationale for the programs also changed. Although the MDBs had been established as public financial intermediaries to remedy imperfections in world capital markets unprepared to lend to war-devastated countries or remote, unknown parts of the globe, the soft loan windows were aid vehicles like the U.S. government's direct bilateral foreign aid program. By the mid-1990s, the net disbursements being provided by the MDBs in the form of concessional loans to the poorer countries exceeded the transfers provided on hard terms to the wealthier countries.[1]

The uses of MDB funds from both the hard and soft loan windows also broadened. Cold War security concerns impelled the Western allies, led by the United States, to want to provide resources to some countries faster than traditional MDB infrastructure construction programs allowed. Likewise, both security concerns and humanitarian interests led to large MDB transfers to developing country governments for programs such as integrated rural development and urban development. These programs were intended to permit recipient governments to undertake investments to improve the incomes and living conditions of disadvantaged groups, thereby reducing the likelihood that they would support communist insurgents. Although the MDBs generally have not funded humanitarian relief (that is, food and other aid that is meant to be directly consumed to meet an immediate humanitarian need), beginning in the 1970s, they have devoted sizable funding to investment programs intended to benefit poor groups (for example, credit, land titling, and extension services for poor farmers, improvements in urban shelter for the poor, and many types of expenditures for health, population, and education programs).

The early 1980s brought two more expansions in the types of programs funded by the MDBs. Although program loans, or financial transfers for general budget support, had been made previously, the amount of such lending was greatly increased during the 1980s. The theory was that if this funding were available from the MDBs (as well as from the World Bank's international monetary counterpart, the International Monetary Fund), it would induce developing country governments to adopt better economic, financial, and sectoral policies, provided that the lending was accompanied by appropriate policy reform conditions. MDB loans were also used to support various types of debt work-out programs agreed between borrowing governments and their private creditors during the international debt crisis of the 1980s.

Another type of MDB activity that was greatly expanded during the 1980s was lending in direct support of private projects. Consistent with the U.S. administration's strong support for the private sector, the World Bank dramatically expanded the programs of its small specialized affiliate, the International Finance Corporation (IFC), to take equity positions and provide loans on nearly commercial terms to private enterprises in the developing world. For these investments, developing country governments did not provide guarantees as they did for other World Bank programs. The regional development banks quickly established similar programs. In 1988, the World Bank Group further expanded with the U.S.-led creation of a Multilateral Investment Guarantee Agency (MIGA) to provide a multilateral official source of political risk insurance for private projects.

The newest type of MDB entity to be created was the Global Environment Facility (GEF), a multilateral mechanism to provide grants to address four types of global environmental problems. This entity, although managed by its own secretariat and governing bodies, is headquartered at the World Bank, and U.S. government participation is managed much as it is in the four official World Bank Group entities.

Two of the four regional development banks evolved somewhat differently. The African Development Bank (AfDB), established in Abidjan by the African nations themselves in 1964, only welcomed non-African members in 1982. However, it had created its concessional lending window in 1972 to which the developed countries, including the United States, contributed before they became bank members.

The European Bank for Reconstruction and Development (EBRD) was the brainchild of French president François Mitterrand

and his adviser Jacques Attali, who desired a European-led institution to help reintegrate Central and Eastern Europe into the European mainstream. Although initially cool to the idea, the United States eventually became the largest shareholder and shaped the direction of the institution in a way that differed in key features from the older MDBs. The EBRD, headquartered in London, is required to lend 60 percent or more of its resources to private sector or privatizing entities and can lend only to countries moving toward democracy. It does not have a concessional lending window.

By the end of the 1990s the "MDB system" had grown dramatically, both through planned expansion to incorporate the desire of someone—often the U.S.—for it to undertake a new function and through buildup of financial resources, as the decades of hard window lending generated huge reflows of loan principal and sizable amounts of net income. (MDB net income is used to pay administrative costs of the institution, to establish reserves, and in some cases is transferred to the soft loan affiliate to expand the resources available for concessional lending.) In table 1-1, data derived from recent annual reports of the MDBs show the total subscribed capital of each MDB window/affiliate and the amount of resources each committed to developing countries in a recent year. (The various MDBs have different limitations on the amount of subscribed capital that is considered usable.)

Clearly, the "MDB system" is now large, complex, and powerful. It is providing developing countries with more than $50 billion in new loan and equity commitments annually. (Note that these figures are for gross annual MDB commitments, which may be quite different from the net disbursements used in comparing official transfers with various types of private flows, discussed later.) Not only has the size of MDB programs grown substantially, but the relative importance of these programs as a part of the official U.S. relationship with developing countries has grown even more.

The relative role of the U.S. bilateral aid program is perceived by many to have been declining for a number of years, while funding for bilateral economic aid has declined substantially in recent years to about $8.6 billion in FY 1999[2] (see table 1-2 for funding commitments since World War II). Of this amount, more than $1.8 billion is used for economic support for Israel and Egypt. Bilateral aid has declined for numerous reasons, including the inability of several administrations to agree with Congress on aid priorities; the perceived greater cost effectiveness of multilateral

TABLE 1-1
Total Subscribed Capital and Annual Commitments of the MDBs, FY 1998
(Millions of U.S. dollars)

	Total Subscribed Capital	*Annual Commitments*
The World Bank Group		
IBRD (Hard loan window)	$186,436	$21,086
IDA (Soft loan window)	95,055[a]	7,508
IFC (Private sector affiliate)	2,336	2,718[b]
MIGA (Export insurance)	1,079	831[c]
GEF[d] (Global environmental projects)	5,558	363[e]
The African Development Bank		
AfDB (Hard loan window)	22,375	932[f]
AfDF (Soft loan window)	13,092	810
The Asian Development Bank		
ADB (Hard loan window)	48,500	4,995
ADF (Soft loan window)	20,535[g]	987
The Inter-American Development Bank		
OC (Hard loan window)	94,219	9,364
FSO (Soft loan window)	9,643[h]	686
IIC (Private sector affiliate)	203	223[i]
MIF (New grant facility)	1,066[j]	137

TABLE 1-1 *(continued)*

	Total Subscribed Capital	*Annual Commitments*
The European Bank for Reconstruction and Development		
EBRD	21,285[k]	2,207[k]
(Government and private sector hard loan window)		

Source: 1998 annual reports of each institution and information supplied by GEF officers.

[a]Subscriptions and contributions committed by members.

[b]Includes loans and equity investments.

[c]Contingent liability guarantees.

[d]Although the GEF is not officially part of the World Bank, for U.S. oversight purposes it is managed much like the four World Bank entities.

[e]Largely grants.

[f]Includes loans and grants, private equity investments, emergency operations, and loan reallocations.

[g]Total resources.

[h]Total contributions.

[i]Loans and equity investments.

[j]Total assets.

[k]Based on ECU conversion rate of $1 = 1.1034 on June 18, 1998.

aid, especially the MDBs; and, at times, poor leadership at the U.S. Agency for International Development (USAID). Funding provided to developing countries through UN agencies has declined also. In addition to MDB financial commitments forming a larger part of U.S.-supported transfers to developing countries, the United States has encouraged the MDBs to assume functions that in earlier eras would have been performed by U.S. agencies directly. The United States has elected to support MDB leadership for even such politically delicate chores as coordinating reconstruction in Bosnia and Kosovo and managing a trust fund to support economic development in the West Bank and Gaza strip.

Data in table 1-3 reflect the growing relative importance both of the concessional windows of the MDBs compared with the non-concessional windows, and also the relative decline of UN aid programs compared with those of the MDBs. (Net disbursements

TABLE 1-2
U.S. Funding for Economic Aid, Not Including MDB Funding, 1946–1997
(Millions of constant FY 1998 U.S. dollars)[a]

Year	*Amount*	*Year*	*Amount*
1946	$25,856	1973	$14,394
1949	63,783	1976[b]	15,783
1952	15,633	1979	15,587
1955	14,867	1982	13,557
1958	13,563	1985	18,522
1961	17,472	1988	12,315
1964	20,071	1991	14,281
1967	18,181	1994	13,064
1970	14,769	1997	9,377

Source: Congressional Research Service Database, June 4, 1999.
[a]This chart shows bilateral economic aid funding but also includes relatively small amounts appropriated for voluntary U.S. contributions to various UN agencies.
[b]Includes transition quarter as the United States changed its fiscal year starting date.

are presented to compare the impact of funds provided on a variety of different repayment terms.)

A More Difficult and Complex Mission

In their early years the MDBs benefited from a clear mandate that they were well equipped to fulfill—financial intermediation to overcome imperfections in capital markets that failed to channel sufficient resources to substantial parts of the world. To this was gradually added another mandate that the MDBs could also accomplish with relative ease—the channeling of large sums to countries and governments judged worthy of support for Cold War reasons.

Not only were these mandates relatively easy for the MDBs to fulfill, they were also quite easy for the United States to make decisions about and monitor. There were arguments, at times heated ones, among different elements in the U.S. government and between the United States and other MDB members about which countries, regions, or sectors should receive more resources at the margin. There were also disagreements about the total amount the

TABLE 1-3
Net Disbursements of Concessional and Nonconcessional Flows by Multilateral Aid Organizations
(Millions of U.S. dollars; net disbursements at current prices and exchange rates)

	1970–1971	*1980*	*1990*	*1993*	*1996*	*1997*
Concessional flows						
Multilateral development banks						
International Development Association	$225	$1,543	$3,912	$4,470	$5,723	$5,253
Inter-American Development Bank Concessional Funds	219	326	155	88	405	292
African Development Fund	—	96	603	683	591	589
Asian Development Fund	3	149	1,101	954	1,102	1,010
Subtotal	**447**	**2,114**	**5,771**	**6,195**	**7,821**	**7,144**
United Nations aid agencies						
World Food Program	125	539	933	1,488	1,082	1,072
UN Development Program	219	660	1,130	1,201	1,469	1,627
UN High Commissioner for Refugees	8	465	466	1,259	833	703
UNICEF	47	247	584	798	677	656
Other UN	130	577	1,385	1,501	1,207	825
Subtotal	**529**	**2,488**	**4,498**	**6,247**	**5,268**	**4,883**
IMF[a]	—	1,636	321	189	330	178
European Community	208	1,061	2,843	3,882	5,261	5,156
Total concessional	**1,184**	**7,299**	**13,433**	**16,513**	**18,680**	**17,361**

Nonconcessional flows						
Multilateral development banks						
IBRD	585	3,166	5,009	1,526	(238)	3,145
IFC	62	295	1,385	1,017	3,096	—
IDB	104	567	1,060	2,081	1,409	2,697
AfDB	4	97	1,001	1,074	291	(33)
ADB	29	328	1,197	1,239	218	3,971
EBRD	—	—	—	6	377	244
Subtotal	**784**	**4,453**	**9,652**	**6,943**	**5,153**	**10,024**
European Community	34	257	299	343	303	836
Total nonconcessional	**818**	**4,710**	**9,951**	**7,286**	**5,456**	**10,860**

Source: OECD statistics contained in *Development Cooperation: Development Assistance Committee 1998 Report*, 1999 edition (Paris: OECD, 1999), A42, and *Development Cooperation* (Paris: OECD, 1992), A38. For simplicity, small flows from several additional organizations were omitted.

Note: This table covers concessional and nonconcessional flows to countries on part 1 of DAC list of aid recipients (includes almost all developing countries).

[a]IMF Trust fund, SAF, and ESAF.

United States should contribute to the MDBs in a particular year. However, the basic purpose of and need for the MDBs were not questioned seriously in the United States.

Likewise, the performance of the institutions was quite easy to monitor because it largely involved checking on whether funds went to the approved countries. In this era MDB and U.S. officials routinely used the ratio of MDB funds transferred to borrowers, compared with MDB administrative expenses, as a measure of institutional efficiency and success.

By the 1990s, the environment in which the MDBs operated had changed. International capital markets had grown enormously in size and interest in providing funding for lucrative opportunities throughout the world. Countries that were perceived to be pursuing sound policies were able to secure substantial private funding, and in some cases funders were willing to overlook major policy flaws if other aspects of the investment were sufficiently enticing. Specialized investment vehicles that were more suited to developing country risks had been devised. Although official development finance from Western governments was declining about 10 percent in net terms from 1991 to 1997, net flows from private sources increased more than fivefold—from about $50 billion to more than $250 billion (see table 1-4). Net disbursements from the MDBs remained quite stable, ranging from about $13 billion to about $17 billion.

Although the 1997–1998 global economic crisis produced a decline in private flows of about 11 percent in 1997, by the spring of 1999 there were numerous reports of renewed access to private markets by even the more severely affected countries. There also were some indications that the crisis had spurred private investors to develop more in-depth knowledge of developing country borrowers and, hence, greater ability to differentiate among borrowers and provide financing on terms deemed more commensurate with risk.[3] Clearly, the lack of interest in soundly performing developing countries on the part of private sources of capital—the problem that had sparked the creation of the MDBs—had changed significantly.

The 1997 authorized history of the World Bank recognizes the change in circumstances that has eroded the need for the MDBs as classic financial intermediaries and the subsequent implicit shift in their raison d'etre.

> One of the authors of the World Bank's first authorized history [written in 1973] was preoccupied with whether the Bank would be able to "change its spots" from being mostly a bank

TABLE 1-4
Total Net Resource Flows from OECD Member Countries and Multilateral Agencies to Aid Recipients
(Billions of current U.S. dollars)

	1981	*1991*	*1993*	*1996*	*1997(p)*[a]
Official development finance	**$45.5**	**$84.8**	**$83.4**	**$78.1**	**$76.8**
Official aid[b]	**36.8**	**64.0**	**61.9**	**63.6**	**55.1**
Bilateral	28.9	46.3	44.6	43.1	36.0
Multilateral	7.9	17.7	17.3	20.5	19.1
Other official development finance[c]	**8.7**	**20.8**	**21.5**	**14.5**	**21.7**
Bilateral	3.0	13.1	11.4	5.8	5.9
Multilateral	5.7	7.7	10.1	8.7	15.8
Export credits	**16.2**	**0.6**	**(3.0)**	**4.0**	**(4.4)**
Private flows	**74.3**	**50.8**	**81.9**	**282.7**	**252.1**
Direct investment	17.2	23.2	38.4	63.5	107.8
International bank lending[d]	52.3	10.7	4.8	86.0	20.0
Total bond lending	1.3	4.9	28.7	93.8	91.2
Other, including equities[e]	1.5	6.6	4.3	33.8	28.5
Grants by nongovernmental organizations	2.0	5.4	5.7	5.6	4.6
Total net resource flows	**136.0**	**136.2**	**162.3**	**364.8**	**324.5**

Source: OECD statistics contained in *Development Cooperation: Development Assistance Committee 1998 Report,* 1999 edition (Paris: OECD, 1999), A1-2, and *Development Cooperation* (Paris: OECD, 1990), 123.

Note: Table does not include interest paid by aid recipients or net use of IMF credits.

[a]Provisional.

[b]Includes both official development assistance (ODA) and official aid, which are concessional assistance to poorer and to more developed countries respectively. Excludes forgiveness of non-ODA debt for 1991.

[c]Assistance provided on less concessional terms.

[d]Excludes bond lending by banks and government-guaranteed financial credits (included in export credits).

[e]Reporting by several countries is incomplete.

> to mostly a development agency. That question is no longer widely contested; the Bank, without abandoning some of its bankerly attributes, is generally credited with having become, not just a, but the, leading development agency of its time.[4]

At about the same time, the end of the Cold War decreased the perceived need of the Western allies to provide resources to buttress friendly regimes. Therefore, with the motivation diminishing to transfer resources to developing countries for containing communism or to remedy capital market imperfections, the spotlight turned to the concrete accomplishments of the loans provided by the MDBs and other taxpayer-supported sources of finance to developing countries.

By the early 1990s, a substantial body of material had been produced on the results of the wide array of official financial transfers to developing countries. These studies differed greatly in methodology, in coverage, in findings, and in interpretation of results.[5] However, the conclusions clearly did not bear out the once prevalent assumption—that simply transferring resources to poor countries would predictably lead to increased economic growth, development, poverty reduction, and perhaps even political pluralism and democracy. Similarly, there were doubts in a number of cases that politically motivated transfers had succeeded in establishing lasting and valuable political ties. Therefore, in the future it would be difficult for official financial and aid institutions to justify their continuance, let alone their growth, primarily on their skill at transferring resources. Instead, they would need to show that those resources had accomplished desirable objectives.

The World Bank itself recently concluded: "Foreign aid has concentrated too much on the transfer of capital. . . . Disbursements. . . were easily calculated and tended to become a critical output measure for development institutions. Agencies saw themselves as being primarily in the business of dishing out money, so it is not surprising that much went into poorly managed economies—with little result."[6]

In recent years a heated debate has been initiated, especially in the United States, about whether the MDBs and other taxpayer-supported transfers to developing countries are still needed in light of the significant increase in potentially available private capital. Examination of this issue concerning the MDBs was the primary purpose of the first phase of the project under which this study was undertaken by the Center for Strategic and International Studies.

A broad-based CSIS task force concluded that the MDBs should not fund projects for which private funding is available or would be available if the borrowing country pursued appropriate policies, unless there is clear evidence that externalities or market failure justify the use of MDB resources. This would appear particularly to reduce the instances in which the multilateral banks' financial intermediation function would be appropriate, because changes in capital markets have greatly reduced the instances in which potentially profitable projects cannot be financed on capital markets if the country's policies are adequate for project success.

The MDBs' unique qualities as multilateral public-sector institutions, which can link conceptual work with funding, enable them to play an important role as purveyors of technical and policy advice, as conveners of diverse groups, and as sources of funding for projects that have potentially high economic and social returns but for which financial returns are insufficient to attract private resources. The task force thought that the MDBs should place more emphasis on developing the institutional, regulatory, and policy framework for private sector development and for safeguarding the public interest from corrupt distortions of it.

The group also believed that the MDBs should play a significant role in grappling with the pervasive problem of poverty in the developing world. The task force thought the MDBs could be especially effective in poverty reduction by leveraging better borrower policies in this area and by providing technical assistance and funding, when needed, for programs that increased the productive capacity of the poor, especially small business, microenterprise, and small agricultural producers. The group was concerned that the MDBs not fund programs for which the type of resources they could provide, in most cases hard currency loans, were not suitable. The task force had strong differences of view over the extent to which the MDBs should provide funding or guarantees for private sector projects.[7]

Most of the functions put forward as important tasks for the MDBs now are much more complex and difficult to carry out successfully than those the institutions performed in their early years. Also, they require the institutions to exercise greater judgment than in the past about the circumstances in which particular activities are appropriate.

Specific functions for which many believe the MDBs are still needed include

- helping developing countries to formulate legal and regulatory frameworks in areas like competition policy, environmental protection, and financial institution standards. These issues often are controversial and complex, and the attainment of objectives usually involves challenging powerful local interests.

• strengthening local institutions to fulfill many functions—from overseeing electric utilities to enforcing banking regulations. In most cases the roadblocks to satisfactory institutional performance extend beyond a lack of funding and involve difficult social and political issues.

• helping to design and finance socially desirable investments that are not attractive to private funding, such as education, health, and environmental programs. To be successful these programs need to be acceptable to those who use them, accurately targeted on those who need them, and sustainable after MDB funding has ended.

• providing advice on improved borrower policies and financing to facilitate their implementation—but only after careful consideration of whether the reforms are significant enough to produce results, are supported by local stakeholders and, therefore, likely to be implemented, and whether external resources will be helpful or counterproductive to a reform process.

• serving as a catalyst for private capital flows—without going too far and providing unjustified subsidies to private groups.

Not only are these tasks difficult to accomplish even in developed countries (for example, recent debates in the United States over environmental standards, antitrust policy, and welfare reform), but they require a much wider range of expertise than has been required in the past. In addition, most of these functions are not those of banks, but of development agencies, consulting firms, regulatory agencies, and even venture capitalists.

The MDBs under Fire

How the MDBs have addressed these less universally agreed and more difficult functions has been criticized from many quarters. Conservative groups have long charged that the MDBs encourage too large a role for the public sector, compete with private financiers to fund potentially profitable projects, and lend to corrupt and dictatorial regimes. Recent MDB programs to directly support private projects especially have been criticized as interfering with markets and providing unjustified subsidies to both private firms and developing country governments. Ian Vasquez of the Cato Institute wrote about a recent World Bank–IDB loan for a gas pipeline in Brazil: "If the lending agencies are not supplanting sources of private finance, then they are second guessing the market's judgment about the financial worthiness of such investments."[8]

The MDBs have been criticized by those on various points of the ideological spectrum for being ineffective and secretive bureaucracies that make large loans even when the borrowers' policies are not adequate to use them productively. Many observers have criticized the MDBs, along with other institutions, for failing to recognize or take decisive action on the policy failings in developing countries that gave rise to recent financial crises. In testimony before Congress, the former general counsel of the Inter-American Development Bank asked: "How can it be that Mexico, before the 1994 peso devaluation, and Indonesia, most recently, have been described by the World Bank as 'star' performers, and that the crisis, requiring billions of dollars in bail-out money, comes upon the IMF and the World Bank as a surprise?"[9] The *Financial Times* similarly noted:

> Indonesia has been consistently praised for its sensible macro-economic and monetary policies. But the weaknesses have been at the micro-economic level: in the explosion of ill-regulated banks, and the concentration of business and political power in the hands of a tiny elite, unaccountable to any but the 76-year-old president. Institutions like the IMF, the World Bank, and the Asian Development Bank, not to mention friendly governments, have failed to spell out the dangers of such weaknesses in good time.[10]

Even more recently similar questions have been raised about the role of the EBRD in Russia. The *Wall Street Journal* noted:

> With its undeniable clout, some private-sector bankers and banking analysts argue, the EBRD should have done more to pressure Moscow to put in place sound economic policies. The bank also has been criticized for its handling of the collapse of Tokobank, a Russian bank in which the EBRD held a minority stake, whose bankruptcy in May was a harbinger of Russia's broader financial crisis.[11]

Most surprising, perhaps, is the blistering critique that has been levied at the MDBs by some of the staunchest advocates of development aid. A wide spectrum of U.S. nongovernmental organizations (NGOs) that are active on development or environmental issues, supported by mainstream U.S. foundations, have been strongly critical of the MDBs' activities for more than 10 years and remain so today. A number of these groups banded together in the "Fifty Years Is Enough" coalition in 1994 in observance of the fiftieth anniversary of the Bretton Woods Conference that drew up plans for the World Bank. The critiques of this group have been laid out in detail in a series of books published by mainstream publishers in the last several years.[12]

According to this group's major criticisms, MDB programs do not effectively reduce poverty, do not respond to the perceptions and wishes of those they purport to help, and do not reflect enough concern for human rights or governance issues. MDB projects damage the environment, and frequent promises to fix problems or support beneficial initiatives have not materialized. In another frequent theme, MDB actions, especially on the ground in developing countries, are not consistent with their stated policies, and the institutions seek to hide these discrepancies behind restrictive confidentiality policies that limit public access to their key operating documents.

Although the multilateral banks contend that they have progressed toward remedying the problems their critics have identified, a brief review of reports published since the beginning of 1997 by a variety of groups helps to explain the continuing public ambivalence toward these institutions:

- One of the rare independent reports commissioned by a multilateral institution itself reported the following about a troubled IFC project in Chile and what it revealed about the institution's operations:

> The single most important conclusion of this performance audit was that IFC did not follow fundamental World Bank Group requirements in any consistent or comprehensible manner. . . . A basic system of accountability requires both that there are understood organizational objectives and that they are based on rigorous processes rather than retrospective self-evaluation for determining whether those objectives were consistently obtained. As noted above, clearly understood organizational standards of performance are absent at IFC.[13]

- In a July 21, 1997, report on MDB environmental performance, the Congressional Research Service wrote:

> Recent preliminary investigations by the [World Bank's Inspection] Panel substantiate complaints that environmental and social elements included in [World Bank] loan agreements are not always carried out. According to one observer, it can too often be the case that once a loan is approved, the bank in question considers the matter closed and "moves on to other things," with little on-going supervision and little effort to assure that environmental and other conditions or requirements are being met.[14]

• Various nongovernmental groups expressed strong public concern about the World Bank's performance in a number of areas. The Lawyers Committee for Human Rights was so concerned about a draft World Bank handbook on laws in developing countries concerning NGOs, it widely disseminated a special report that concluded: "The Handbook, as currently written, is inconsistent in fundamental respects with basic principles of the international law of freedom of association. . . ."[15] Similarly, the Bank Information Center concluded a 1998 report about a large World Bank–IDB project in South America, "Fundamentally, the [World] Bank culture rewards staff for loaning money and convincing governments to borrow for projects, but does not admonish them for causing harm, even if that harm has enormous environmental, social, or economic consequences or results in project failure. . . . There are no incentives for Bank staff to comply with policies, or consequences if they don't."[16]

• The NGO Population Action International, reported in 1997 on World Bank activities in its areas of interest in *Falling Short: The World Bank's Role in Population and Reproductive Health*:

> The quality of [World Bank] project design has also been an issue. . . . While Bank projects across all sectors suffer from deficiencies in design, the complexity of HNP [health, nutrition, population] projects make them more vulnerable to design-related implementation problems. . . . Frequent and effective monitoring remains critical to the successful implementation of social sector activities, including complex HNP projects. Yet supervision of population activities has been another major stumbling bloc for the Bank.[17]

• Yet another set of criticisms were levied at the World Bank in the *Far Eastern Economic Review* by a professor of political economy from Northwestern University who has long worked in Southeast Asia:

> Everyone has heard the horror stories of World Bank projects gone wrong: environmental loans that pave the Southeast Asian rain forest, industrial loans based on whimsical price forecasts in China, poverty-alleviation projects that evict the poor from their homes in India. The World Bank's high priests of market reform would have us believe these are just the hiccups on an otherwise healthy organism.
>
> But the World Bank is really two organizations, and that smooth message. . . . comes from what I call the Rhetorical Bank. Meanwhile, top management inside the patronage machine known as the Real Bank is aware that these stories are symptoms of a much graver disease.
>
> . . . The more money staffers move, the more status they have within the Real Bank. . . . While the Real Bank busily funds bureaucracy and turns a blind eye to waste and exploitation, the Rhetorical Bank calls incessantly for deregulation, smaller government, and an end to subsidies.
>
> . . . The costs are born by poor countries. The World Bank resident office in Jakarta, for example, admits that 30% of the money lent to Indonesia routinely disappears somewhere inside the government.[18]

• More recently the *Wall Street Journal* examined in greater detail the World Bank's role in the Indonesia meltdown:

> Not only did the development agency [the World Bank] lend money and credibility to Gen. Suharto, but critics say it tolerated and in some ways may have inadvertently stoked the corruption and economically corrosive practices that increasingly characterized the Suharto regime in recent years. . . .
>
> The bank, at the government's insistence, softened reports on Indonesia's economy, reports that helped the government win better ratings and draw in capital. When the economy got dicey last year, this capital fled, undermining Indonesia's currency.
>
> The World Bank lent $307 million to replenish the capital of state-run banks, which then channeled much of that money to companies run by Mr. Suharto's cronies. It was the failure of those same companies to repay earlier loans that had necessitated the state-bank recapitalization.[19]

Finally, one of the staunchest supporters of the MDBs, Senator Patrick Leahy, voiced the concern of many of the sympathetic observers when he told the Senate on November 13, 1997:

> [By appropriating funds to clear previous U.S. arrears to the World Bank] we are sending the message that we expect this investment to yield results. We are fortunate that World Bank President Wolfensohn is a dynamic and reform-minded leader. . . . Frankly, I am concerned that despite his best intentions, the Bank bureaucracy continues to put up fierce resistance and may in the end succeed in thwarting many of his reforms.[20]

Given the criticism of MDB operations from a range of sources, it is hardly surprising that U.S. support for the MDBs has been inconsistent in recent years.

Although some have attributed the fall in popularity of the MDBs and some other government foreign aid programs as a "turning inward" by Americans after the end of the Cold War, others attribute the lack of popularity of these programs to more specific doubts on the part of many Americans about their effectiveness. A Harvard University researcher on foreign aid pointed out several years ago that U.S. public opinion was divided between a desire to help needy people in developing countries and a lack of support for U.S. government foreign aid programs—a divide he attributed to a lack of confidence that U.S. aid programs were working.[21] A report published in 1997 by the University of Maryland quoted a finding of three recent surveys that Americans "were frustrated with the performance of foreign aid programs," rather than opposing the concept of foreign aid.[22] More serious than the loss of public support, according to another recent study, is that foreign aid has lost its "salience and credibility within the [U.S.] foreign policy establishment."[23]

Against this backdrop of specific criticism of MDB performance and general public concern about the efficacy of all foreign aid, Congress, led by members of both parties, but advancing different arguments, has failed to support MDB funding requests. The first move came in 1993 when the House Banking subcommittee under the chairmanship of a strong foreign aid supporter, Representative Barney Frank, took the unprecedented step of denying the World Bank's concessional lending affiliate, the International Development Association (IDA) its requested three-year authorization. Instead, the subcommittee authorized IDA funding for two years and made authorization for the third year contingent on the institution's performance in designated areas. Although U.S. NGOs had pressed for MDB reforms in the past, this action was the first time they and their supporters in Congress had actually delayed a funding request to try to obtain changes. A few months later when control of the Congress shifted to the Republicans, they sharply cut back funding for the MDBs citing concerns about lack of transparency and excessive MDB support for public sector programs.

These large cuts triggered sharp protests from developed country allies as well as an attempt to block U.S. firms from obtaining contracts under the World Bank programs to which U.S. contributions were delayed. The international protests, as well as the different Republican justifications for the cuts, to some extent drove the NGO critics of the multilateral development banks to declare that they supported full U.S. funding for the institutions in order to maintain U.S. standing to press for internal changes. At the same time, the Clinton administration, concerned about the foreign reaction to both MDB and UN funding shortfalls, made foreign affairs funding one of its top three priorities in the government-wide budget negotiations in the spring of 1997 and negotiated agreement that payment of already agreed contributions to international financial institutions would not be counted against the totals allowed under the budget limits.[24]

The Clinton administration's unusual step of ranking foreign aid funding so high on its list of overall priorities, combined with the concerted campaign of a number of groups that had been alarmed by the dimensions of previous congressional cuts, proved strong enough to pass appropriations that made up U.S. funding shortfalls to the MDBs when the FY 1998 budget was passed in November 1997. However, similar efforts to make up shortfalls to the UN and to provide funding for the International Monetary Fund (IMF) were not approved. During deliberations on the FY 1999 budget, almost all attention was focused on the controversial IMF funding request, which was approved only in the final hours of the congressional session.

There is no evidence, however, that MDB critics have changed their minds about the need for, or performance record of, these institutions. Indeed, the FY 1999 appropriations legislation required the creation of a commission, all the members of which would be selected by majority and minority leaders in Congress, to examine the "future role and responsibilities of the international financial institutions" including "possible mergers or abolition" of some of them.[25] In addition, Congress continues to closely track examinations of possible corruption in the use of MDB funds. Also, there is no sign that NGO concerns about the problems in the MDBs have lessened. One of the major NGO spokesmen on the MDBs concluded a report on the World Bank for an academic conference in May 1999 with the following summary:

> World Bank actions under Wolfensohn increasingly have revealed a pattern. The charismatic, passionate President makes spectacular personal gestures and supports worthy but peripheral institutional commitments to please the Bank's politically correct constituencies. Often there is little follow-through, and little to no significant impact on operations. . . . The deepest, strongest bureaucratic pull in the direction of the "culture of loan approval" is fatally reinforced. The octopus-like bureaucracy emits an immense ink cloud of reports that for 20 years have identified the same problems, but the reports like all their predecessors have no lasting operational consequences. . . . Meanwhile the institution risks mutating into an entity for which public support may be harder and harder to justify.[26]

Recent budget agreements bought time and a temporary truce on MDB funding, but underlying disagreements about the role of multilateral development banks and the quality of their performance remain unresolved.

2

Formulating U.S. Policy toward the MDBs: A Bare-Bones, Stand-Alone System

The multilateral development banks, as independent international organizations, are run by their own managements. Because they are owned by member governments, policy direction and oversight responsibility are exercised by those member governments. The governing structures of all of the MDBs provide for ultimate decisions to be made by a board of governors representing all member countries, which usually meets once a year. Operations of the institutions are supervised by boards of executive directors, also representing member governments, that meet frequently and approve all projects and policies.

When formal votes are required, members have voting power that is related to their financial contribution to the institution's hard loan window. U.S. voting power in the five MDBs is shown in table 2-1, along with that of the other large shareholders for comparison purposes. Most decisions are taken by majority vote, but in practice the countries providing the bulk of financial resources wield disproportionate power.

Each member country manages its participation in these institutions differently. The United States, as the largest shareholder in all but one of the banks, has an easier situation than other countries because it has the right to name its own executive director in each institution, whereas other countries, with lower voting power, usually must group together, with one executive director representing several countries.

Under the terms of the Bretton Woods Act, passed by Congress when the World Bank was established in 1945, the U.S. governor

TABLE 2-1
Voting Power of Largest Shareholders in the MDBs

Country	*Percent of Total Vote*	*Country*	*Percent of Total Vote*
World Bank		***Inter-American Development Bank***	
United States	17.03	United States	31.11
Japan	6.04	Argentina	10.95
Germany	4.67	Brazil	10.95
France	4.47	Mexico	7.04
United Kingdom	4.47	Venezuela	5.87
Asian Development Bank		***African Development Bank***	
United States	13.20	Nigeria	10.00
Japan	13.20	Egypt	5.77
China	5.66	United States	5.61
India	5.57	Cote d'Ivoire	5.02
Australia	5.12	Japan	4.63
EBRD			
United States	10.91		
Japan	9.32		
Germany	9.32		
United Kingdom	9.32		
France	9.32		

Source: 1997 Annual Report data.

of the World Bank is the same individual who serves as the U.S. governor of the International Monetary Fund (IMF), specified by the president as the secretary of the Treasury. This act was amended when the United States joined each of the regional banks to provide for the same structure for each institution. The U.S. executive director in each bank is appointed by the president and reports to the secretary of the Treasury through the assistant secretary for international affairs.[1]

The U.S. Congress must approve all new U.S. funding for the MDBs. Additions to U.S. callable capital subscriptions must be approved by Congress but are not included as items requiring "budget authority" in the federal budget (given the expectation that they will never need to be transferred to the institution).

Underlying Assumptions

The way the United States manages its participation in the MDBs has changed remarkably little over the years. In many aspects the U.S. policy process still reflects key assumptions from the institutions' early years.

The first assumption that still guides U.S. participation is faith that if an appropriate management structure can be put in place in the institutions, only relatively light oversight of institutional performance from member governments is required. This assumption guides both the level and the type of resources the United States devotes to such oversight. Believers in this assumption often list reduction in U.S. management burdens as an advantage of aid provided through the MDBs and other multilateral institutions.

Catherine Caufield noted this assumption concerning the World Bank in her recent book: "It is taken for granted [by Bank executive directors] that management would not propose a project that is technically, financially, or otherwise unsound."[2]

The second assumption that has long guided U.S. participation in the MDBs is that their basic role and mission is agreed upon. The policy process is not geared to dealing with serious disagreement about the role of the institutions or to making far-reaching changes. It is not structured in a way likely to engender initiatives for the institutions to pare back or drop existing functions.

Third, the U.S. policy process implicitly reflects the assumption that institutional achievements will be directly related to the quantity of inputs or funds expended, because U.S. efforts to monitor the activities of the MDBs are based on monitoring and tracking inputs. The United States looks at how much money flows from which MDB to which country for which stated purpose. The United States reviews, at least cursorily, all MDB project proposals describing how the institution plans to use resources. It does not devote remotely comparable effort to looking at what was actually achieved.

Similarly, the U.S. policy process focuses on official MDB statements of plans and policies. It assumes that MDB actions will follow these statements.[3] In this area executive branch officials differ substantially in perspective from many outside observers and some in Congress. Many critics of the MDBs are concerned that MDB practices in the field often differ greatly from their written policies and official statements.

Congress has tried on several occasions to get the executive branch to pay more attention to the implementation of MDB plans. As early as the 1970s Congress asked the executive branch to report on "the effectiveness of the implementation and administration of the loans made by the [Inter-American Development] Bank based upon the audit reports."[4] Likewise, in 1992 the Senate Appropriations Committee adopted report language urging the U.S. bilateral aid agency to have its field offices in developing countries look into MDB project implementation on the ground, saying: "The Committee is concerned that there is relatively little formal outside oversight for MDB projects once those projects are underway. . . . The result is that intervention usually occurs belatedly, and only when projects are dramatically outside of performance standards."[5] However, neither congressional request resulted in a serious executive branch effort to look at the implementation of MDB programs.

Even when internal MDB evaluations point to persistent problems with project implementation, such as occurred in the "portfolio reviews" done by all of the MDBs (except the new EBRD) in 1992–1994,[6] the United States has chosen to rely on reports of process improvements by the MDBs themselves rather than to adopt a more proactive approach of independently checking on their performance.

Other MDB members have tried at times to take a more hands-on approach. The Danish government commissioned a two-year study of the activities in the field of 11 multilateral organizations, including 3 MDBs, and indicated plans to conduct such reviews regularly, noting: "It is a frequent experience with multilateral development organizations that they adopt a sensible policy in principle, but do not live up to it in practice."[7] The Norwegian government also recently commissioned an independent report on the World Bank's efforts at poverty reduction. However, the current U.S. approach is to rely on reports by the MDBs themselves to assess the effectiveness of their operations and devise measures to remedy problems.

The Process in the Executive Branch

The Major Players

The individuals on the front line of the U.S. relationship with the MDBs are the U.S. executive directors, alternate executive directors, and their staff-level assistants. The U.S. executive director in each of the MDBs normally is a political appointee, chosen by the usual selection process for political appointees and confirmed by the Senate. The alternate executive director position in the larger banks also is usually a political appointment subject to Senate approval. In the newer banks (AfDB and EBRD), the alternate executive director at times is a career Treasury Department officer. At times the United States has chosen not to have an alternate director in these banks for budgetary reasons.

The U.S. executive directors and alternates represent the United States in the MDBs' executive board meetings that consider all projects and policies of the institution. In view of the large sums lent by these institutions, the number and variety of issues considered, and the range of specialized "windows" and "affiliates" that must also be tracked, this is a daunting task. In addition to regular board meetings, the executive directors, who usually work from offices located in the MDBs' headquarters, also attend meetings of board committees to look at more detailed matters, such as the institutions' personnel policies or administrative budgets. They represent the United States to the bank, helping to explain and justify all U.S. actions that affect the institution and its members. They also represent their bank to the gamut of U.S. official and private entities, ranging from U.S. corporations seeking contracts, to U.S. citizens' groups with concerns about bank operations, to U.S. government agencies seeking to collaborate with the bank.

Appointees to U.S. executive director and alternate positions have come from all types of backgrounds, with the greater number having a banking or legal background. Others have been former members of Congress, local officials, academics, and businesspersons.

Each executive director has a small professional staff—usually one or two Treasury Department career staff and an officer from the Commerce Department. The presence of the Commerce officer is mandated by law because Congress was concerned that U.S. businesses were not receiving as much assistance as was being provided by other countries' executive directors in helping to garner contracts under MDB projects. The Commerce Department officers spend their time helping U.S. businesses to understand the complex MDB procurement regulations and procedures. They also check on complaints that U.S. businesses were not treated fairly in specific cases. At times, junior officers from other agencies serve in the U.S. executive directors' offices, but such secondment arrangements have tended to be transitory. This group of about 25 professionals constitutes the official U.S. link with the MDBs.

U.S. executive directors are supposed to take their policy direction from the U.S. governor of the institution, the secretary of the Treasury, or his designee. The attention devoted to the MDBs by the secretary of the Treasury, the deputy secretary, and the under secretary and assistant secretary for international affairs varies greatly, depending on circumstances, personal interests, and the number of other issues on their agendas. In the international arena alone, these officials also must address everything affecting the international economic and financial system and trade, investment, and financial issues between the United States and specific countries. Both historically and by recent accounts, the need to focus on immediately critical international financial issues has drawn much more attention toward the International Monetary Fund and its concerns than is usually given to the MDBs.

For several years, problems in securing congressional funding for the MDBs led Treasury secretary Robert Rubin to spend a significant amount of time on this MDB issue. Many observers contend, however, that usually most MDB issues, especially those concerning the long-term role and impact of the MDBs, are seldom high on the list of concerns of senior Treasury management. This is especially the case for matters that are not primarily economic or financial in nature, such as implementation of MDB projects, the MDBs' skill at strengthening borrower institutions, or the MDBs' treatment of local people in project areas.

Day-to-day matters concerning the MDBs are in the hands of an Office of Multilateral Development Banks that reports, along with the Office of International Debt Policy, to a deputy assistant secretary for international development, debt, and environment policy. The MDB office consists of 15 to 20 professionals—about the size it has been for many years. Of this group, 5 to 7 are "desk officers" for specific MDBs, with 2 officers usually assigned to the World Bank Group. Given the explosion in criticism of the MDBs' environmental performance, 3 officers work in an environment section. Several officers are in charge of reviewing, at least briefly, all of the more than 600 new MDB loan proposals on which the U.S. executive directors must vote each year. One officer works nearly full time on MDB procurement issues, and another is the office's specialist on congressional matters. The office is led by a director who is assisted by two deputies. It is this group that must monitor the performance and do initial thinking on U.S. policy for the growing and embattled MDB system. In contrast, it is estimated that the institutions monitored by this office have combined staffs of 17,000.[8]

The academic training and work experience of the officers in this MDB office are heavily concentrated in economics and finance. Among other reasons, this type background is needed to facilitate career mobility to other positions in the Treasury Department. Exceptions are the officers in the environmental section, who usually have specific training in environmental issues. Because of the emphasis on other qualifications, few members of this office have worked extensively in developing countries. The office's limited funding for staff travel is used for the officers to accompany senior officials to international negotiations on MDB funding, which are usually held in developed countries. It is extremely rare for enough funding to be left over for the Treasury officers to visit developing countries to see MDB projects or to meet with country officials, local residents, or representatives of other aid donors. Likewise, the office has no funding for special studies of new issues or issues requiring specialized expertise. As is the case in many U.S. government agencies, when more senior staff retire or move to other jobs, there is substantial pressure for budgetary reasons to hire more junior and less experienced personnel.[9]

In view of the small size of this group in relation to the issues they must cover, as well as their background in economic theory, it is not surprising that the focus of their efforts, and thus of U.S. official oversight, is the official policy pronouncements of the institutions, especially their economic and financial soundness. Occasionally, Treasury's small cadre of country desk officers, who report up a different management chain of command are also called on to look at an MDB issue, but because this group also tends to be spread very thin, with each officer covering a number of countries, they can devote little time to MDB matters.

The Minor Players

Other Executive Branch Agencies. The State Department is currently the only other executive branch agency that follows MDB issues on a comprehensive and detailed basis. The under secretary of state for economic affairs is the U.S. alternate governor in all of the MDBs, and this role, as well as the State Department's overall responsibility for foreign policy, has always given State influence on some MDB issues. However, the scope and significance of the department's influence varies substantially with the interests and capabilities of its leaders and their relationship with top Treasury officials.

The State Department generally focuses on the effects of MDB issues on U.S. political relationships and tries to monitor all developments to be sure they do not become unnecessary diplomatic irritants. Although the Treasury-State relationship on MDBs has been problematic at times, usually over whether economic or political interests should prevail on particular issues, in recent years Treasury and State have worked together to press Congress for MDB funding and to defend the MDBs from external criticism.

The State Department has a particularly tough challenge with internal coordination regarding the MDBs. Although the department's official link is through the Economic, Business, and Agricultural Affairs Bureau, almost all of State's geographic bureaus have strong interests in the MDBs, as does its Global Affairs unit, which includes bureaus dealing with environmental, population, democracy, and refugee issues. Another State Department unit—the Bureau of International Organization Affairs (IO)—oversees U.S. participation in UN aid agencies. Still another State Department entity is in charge of coordinating the foreign affairs budget request. The fact that at least five different State Department functional bureaus (which relate to three under secretaries), in addition to the geographic bureaus, have interests regarding MDB issues does not make it easy for State to advance substantive proposals on MDB policy.

The Office of Management and Budget (OMB) can be important for U.S. MDB policy, but has not chosen to get much involved in recent years except on specific budget issues. Its influence on MDB matters depends on leaders who have the inclination and political clout to take on senior Treasury Department officials when there are disagreements. One staff member has the responsibility for following all MDBs for OMB, so usually does not have the time or the specialized expertise to look at policy and performance issues in detail.

Like OMB, the National Security Council and the National

Economic Council potentially can affect MDB policy but have generally elected not to do so, or are involved only sporadically on country or regional issues.

The role regarding MDB policy of the U.S. bilateral aid agency, the Agency for International Development (AID), has varied substantially over the years as its fortunes and the interests and capabilities of its leadership have changed. In its early years—the 1960s and early 1970s—AID exerted some influence on MDB policy by virtue of its leaders' intellectual leadership concerning economic development. Several of AID's senior officials from that era went on to become managers in various MDBs.[10]

In the late 1970s the Carter administration, responding to a congressional initiative, devised an ill-fated attempt to bring U.S. bilateral and multilateral aid policy closer together through the creation of the International Development Cooperation Agency (IDCA). IDCA was intended to be a high-level entity (with its director reporting to the president) charged with formulating U.S. policy toward developing countries. It was given oversight responsibility for bilateral aid and U.S. participation in UN development agencies, as well as a substantial role in policymaking toward the MDBs. Stiff Treasury Department resistance to ceding any of its responsibilities toward MDBs caused the final authorities given IDCA regarding the multilateral banks to be quite ambiguous. IDCA's small staff had not carved out a significant role regarding the MDBs when President Carter's defeat in the 1980 election doomed the new agency.

However, the Reagan administration's incoming head of AID, M. Peter McPherson, who also had been given the title of acting director of IDCA, tried for a number of years to utilize the IDCA legal authorities, which were not abolished, to assert a stronger role on MDB policy for AID.[11] McPherson believed that AID must be involved in formulating U.S. policy on the MDBs lest discrepancies between MDB approaches and those of the U.S. bilateral aid program in such areas as policy conditionality, support for the private sector, and provisions for program operating costs damage the efforts of both.

In an effort to expand its role in U.S. policymaking on the MDBs, AID devoted considerable effort for awhile toward getting its sizable offices in developing countries to provide input on upcoming MDB projects and toward a number of other initiatives that AID thought would improve the development aspects of MDB operations. However, AID's efforts at greater involvement often ran into strong Treasury resistance.

As AID's fortunes declined in the 1990s, so did its managers' vision of the agency as a leader in broader development policy areas such as MDB policymaking. In recent years AID has sharply reduced attention to MDB matters as it faced demands for personnel cuts and challenges to its organizational autonomy. Currently AID maintains a computerized system to inform its field missions of future MDB projects and channels any field comments that are routinely generated to Treasury and the U.S. executive directors, but does not especially task its field missions to look at MDB activities, as it did in the 1980s. Likewise, AID does not attempt to keep abreast of key policy issues in the banks or actively try to influence Treasury's response to them.[12]

AID has struggled also to fulfill the congressionally mandated requirement, enacted in 1987, of regularly providing a list of upcoming MDB projects that in its judgment could pose environmental problems. Although AID's leadership has never been enthusiastic about this function, various environmentalists hired on short-term contracts have made serious efforts to generate and analyze as much information as their limited budgets have permitted.[13] Still, a recent Congressional Research Service study concludes: "[AID's] Early Warning System has not been a major source of information."[14]

The Federal Reserve Board is also occasionally involved in MDB policymaking, largely on macroeconomic issues. Its interest in the MDBs reportedly has diminished in the last few years with the resolution of the 1980s debt crisis and the preeminence of the IMF's role in the 1997–1998 global financial crisis.[15]

The Commerce Department, as directed by legislation in 1988, placed a Commerce officer in all U.S. executive directors' offices to help U.S. companies understand the procurement process and get fair treatment in securing MDB contracts. It has not sought, however, to be seriously involved on most other MDB matters.

Several other U.S. government agencies, including the Environmental Protection Agency (EPA), the Department of Agriculture, the Export-Import Bank, the Office of the United States Trade Representative, and the departments of Transportation and Labor, also occasionally have an interest in the MDBs. In some cases a specific staffer is designated to follow MDB matters and to attend the sporadic meetings of an interagency group that looks at MDB projects, but in general these agencies are not involved seriously in U.S. decisionmaking on the MDBs, nor is their specialized expertise harnessed extensively on MDB matters.[16]

Outside Influences. The executive branch has no broad, systematic means of obtaining the views of private U.S. groups as it makes policy toward the MDBs. Outside groups attempting to be heard on MDB issues are addressed individually on an ad hoc basis, with the attention paid their point of view largely dependent on the political influence they can bring to bear. No attempt has been made to bring concerned outside groups together or to articulate how different groups' proposals are or are not consistent with each other. The only regular public interchange the executive branch has with outside groups on MDBs is a monthly meeting, started by AID to help develop its environmental problem project list. In these "Tuesday Group" meetings, NGO representatives meet with AID, Treasury, and State Department environmental staff to exchange information and discuss a variety of NGO concerns. However, the group is attended by relatively low-level staff and has no standing to try to develop a consensus or to make recommendations.[17]

The continuing secrecy of the MDBs, especially on upcoming policy choices, poses problems for outside groups hoping to influence either MDB actions or U.S. policy toward them. Currently the MDBs normally do not make public their major operating documents (that is, their annual budgets, papers on new initiatives, proposed country lending strategies, reports on the status of ongoing projects, et cetera), and the material that is made available is provided only after decisions have been made. This secrecy is an irritant to outside groups interested in the banks and serves to reduce the institutions' popularity with constituencies in the United States that support similar objectives.

Although the executive branch has not taken effective action to significantly change MDB reluctance to make key documents public, the U.S. Congress has had greater success by passing strong legislation. The Pelosi amendment requires as a condition of U.S. support for MDB projects that environmental assessments be available to the public for 120 days before loans are approved by the MDB boards. Although it was limited in scope, concerned groups outside government perceived this congressional requirement as a helpful political signal and a practical step to increase their input to U.S. decisions on the banks and in the MDBs' own deliberations.

In this situation, with the MDBs not encouraging serious public discussion of their future plans, the U.S. policy process addresses public concerns to the degree that it perceives the interested group to have political influence to affect congressional funding for the institutions. Corporations and trade groups differ to the extent they believe their concerns are being satisfactorily addressed. Corporate support is strongly cultivated when the executive branch is concerned about congressional funding, and most corporations can get a hearing from executive branch agencies when they have a specific complaint. Also, beginning in the early 1980s, U.S. executive directors have become more helpful to corporations seeking official U.S. support in matters involving MDB contracts. However, many corporations with a great deal of experience with MDB operations and views about their future role do not perceive that their views are likely to be of interest to government policymakers.[18]

The groups that have made the most intensive and sustained efforts to become involved in the U.S. policy process on MDBs are nongovernmental organizations, especially those interested in environmental and poverty issues. Some of these groups have been extremely influential when the executive branch has perceived that they have strong congressional support and when they have exploited this support with skill. NGOs that lack such Washington "insider" skills have achieved far less influence, and groups that may have an interest but have not mounted a lobbying campaign have no influence on U.S. policy.

Operation of the System

Routine Maintenance. A substantial share of the time the U.S. government devotes to MDBs is spent examining and reacting to the hundreds of MDB project and policy proposals and administrative documents that are produced each year. Almost all of these documents appear as agenda items for the MDB boards of directors' meetings, so the United States traditionally has tried to say something about each of them. These items include more than 600 loan proposals each year, plus country lending strategies for major borrowers in each bank, sector policy papers, administrative budgets, financial status reports, and innumerable special proposals for new activities.

For many years a Treasury Department staffer chaired a weekly interagency meeting to briefly review each loan proposal that would require a U.S. executive director's vote during the next week. Other agencies with an interest in the MDBs sent often relatively junior officers to discuss the upcoming project proposals. Occasionally there were sharp interagency disagreements over U.S. votes. Treasury often wanted to oppose loans that, according to the MDBs' planning documentation, did not meet Treasury's preestablished criteria in economic or financial areas—for example, standards for estimated economic rates of return. The State Department often wanted the United States to be less rigorous about voting against MDB projects, fearing that the negative fallout to the U.S. bilateral relationship with the borrowing country was not worth anything the United States might gain by expressing opposition.

Because U.S. opposition to an MDB loan almost never causes it to be rejected by the institution's executive board and U.S. "no" votes not backed up by other expressions of U.S. displeasure seldom affect an MDB's future actions, the United States recently has ceased to devote as much attention to loan-by-loan scrutiny of proposed MDB projects.[19] The interagency meeting to look at upcoming projects is often canceled now because of a lack of interest from agencies other than Treasury.

U.S. officers working on MDBs also spend a good deal of time reacting and responding to congressional or other criticism of the MDBs. One former manager of the process for the Treasury Department said that he spent about 90 percent of his time drafting senior officials' testimony before Congress and doing "talking points" for other meetings.[20]

For many, the monitoring of MDB activities has proven to be a frustrating exercise. The relatively small staffs are often overwhelmed by the number and variety of documents and issues they are expected to review. A former Nordic executive director at the World Bank wrote:

> With an average tenure of no more than two to three years and with minimal staff support [World Bank] board members had difficulty dealing with the sheer volume, let alone the intricacies, of a vast and complex organization's policies and operations. Thus, in general the board has been no match for the Bank's army of capable and determined managers and staff, and has generally been co-opted or quelled on controversial matters.[21]

The former Venezuelan executive director at the World Bank, Moises Naim, wrote along the same line:

> The volume and complexity of the [World] Bank's work makes it very difficult for directors to be informed and effective participants in all of the discussions where Bank policies and decisions are made. Even though the support staff . . . of executive directors has expanded substantially, and some directors receive additional support from the public agencies in their capitals, the volume and the intricacy of the work have expanded even more.[22]

Not only are the executive directors overwhelmed, so is the small U.S. staff charged with monitoring the banks. According to Catherine Caufield's 1996 book:

> Former U.S. Executive Director Patrick Coady [U.S. executive director at the World Bank, 1989–1993] mourned the fact that most screening of World Bank loans by the U.S. government concerns "U.S. congressional sensitivities or the philosophical tendencies of the administration. I didn't get the support I wish I had in considering whether the actual concept of the loan is good, whether it's going to be implemented properly, whether the disbursement schedules were right, whether the country's underlying policies were appropriate. . . . There was none of that input."[23]

Another more recent former U.S. executive director in a different bank made this point even more strongly, saying he got "no guidance on substance."[24]

In addition to the unavoidable complexity of MDB operations, the banks have adopted a number of procedures that inhibit easy shareholder scrutiny of their operations. Most MDB proposals for policies or projects are only available to executive directors and member governments for 10 to 14 days before the executive board must discuss or vote on them, a quite short period for busy staff to absorb extensive material on complex issues and, if needed, seek policy guidance from higher-level officials. Executive directors may postpone items, but usually only for a few days. These short deadlines pose special difficulties in the case of the United States for the MDBs not headquartered in Washington and cause distant shareholders to have a very hard time monitoring MDB activities.

Most of the MDBs traditionally "bunch" projects and sometimes policy proposals at certain times in their fiscal years, making it even more difficult for thinly stretched executive directors and their governmental authorities to deal with them responsibly.

Some NGOs, especially in the environmental area, have devoted considerable effort to providing U.S. officials with information on MDB projects and policies, which they believe will be helpful to their interests. Information from these groups is often the only "reality check" the U.S. government has about MDB activities. Still, NGOs examine only a small fraction of bank activities and do so from their own perspective, which is not necessarily identical to that of the U.S. government.[25]

If U.S. government officers trying to monitor the activities of the MDBs do not find it an easy task, some believe that their top leadership does not place high priority on this aspect of their work. As Catherine Gwin wrote in her volume, *U.S. Relations with the World Bank, 1945–1992:*

> Although the United States takes credit for fostering stronger audit and evaluation procedures, one might wonder how serious it ever was about project evaluation and impact and whether the poor record on project implementation, documented in the Bank-initiated 1992 Wapenhans Report, would have occurred if the United States had reached a compromise with McNamara in the mid-1970s and addressed the issue of impact consistently.[26]

Some in the NGO community who have long been involved in MDB issues believe that the ministries that provide MDB policy direction do not care greatly about development and project quality issues in the MDBs. The Congressional Research Service study previously quoted noted that on the major issue of whether Secretary Rubin would certify to Congress in 1995 that the IFC was pursuing environmental reforms comparable to those of the rest of the World Bank, Treasury leadership overruled the Treasury's environmental staff to proceed with the certification.[27]

In addition to possible lack of senior-level impetus for proactive scrutiny, U.S. officers trying to examine MDB activities also lack the time and probably the knowledge base to do so adequately. The MDBs are now key actors in an overwhelming array of activities. The areas in which the relevance and quality of their work are most criticized are local implementation, institutional development, regulatory reform, social sector development, private sector finance, governance, human rights, and labor standards—all areas outside the core economic expertise of the group that is supposed to monitor their performance. One veteran observer of MDB activities estimates that the Treasury "doesn't know much about a third to half the issues dealt with by the institutions—that is, the environmental, social, and governance issues."[28] Because many members of this group lack extensive developing country experience and are given few opportunities to gain such experience, they have few options for finding out how MDB activities are working on the ground or how they are perceived by those who are supposed to benefit.

A number of factors lie behind the lack of appropriate expertise to judge MDB activities. The most basic is the assumption that the role of the MDBs is so universally agreed and their ability to perform their functions so clear that more serious scrutiny is not needed. A second factor is the rapid expansion in the scope of the MDBs' work that has far outpaced the evolution of the U.S. policy process. A third factor is the strong preference of the Treasury Department to make MDB decisions without seriously consulting other parts of the executive branch. This tendency makes other agencies reluctant to devote their better expertise to MDB issues because the payout to their involvement in terms of real influence on U.S. policy is perceived to be small.

Policy Development. The U.S. policy development process on MDBs seems to reflect the assumption that fundamental questions on the role and adequate performance of the MDBs have long been settled. Almost all observers describe the U.S. policy development process as ad hoc and reactive, and unlikely to look at issues unless pressed by outside forces—for example, NGO pressure on environment, congressional pressure on various issues, need for additional funding to supplement IMF programs. A recent policy-level official notes that "there wasn't a systematic way of addressing big policies" and that Treasury did not do forward planning on the MDBs.[29] This view is echoed by a key congressional staffer on MDB issues who believes the executive branch "doesn't think long term on MDB matters."[30] A roundtable of former career Treasury officers now serving in various MDBs saw this as failure to think through linkages among issues or to focus enough on matters concerning the institutions' role, rather than concentrating largely on budget requirements.[31] Instead, MDB policy issues are often considered on an individual basis without much attempt to link U.S. positions on them to positions on related issues.

This lack of willingness to look at long-term issues is not new, according to some. A previous Treasury official remembers being concerned about the absence of strategic planning on MDB issues in the late 1970s and successfully recommending the establishment of a new office in Treasury to do such planning on MDB and other developing country matters.[32] However, this office was considered too removed from MDB realities and never succeeded in being seriously involved by policymakers on MDB decisions. It was abolished 10 years later. In the 1980s, negotiations for increased funding for any of the MDBs were considered occasions for a fairly serious review of the institution's performance, but this practice seems to have been dropped or much weakened in recent years.

U.S. policymakers are not perceived as engaged on many of the major questions of the future strategic directions of the MDBs at a time when others, both inside and outside the United States, believe such strategic thinking is needed. In addition, recently the United States has been criticized for strongly pressing the institutions to devote massive resources to short-term rescue operations for relatively wealthy borrowers without giving suitable consideration to the implications for the institutions' financial soundness, longer-term operations, or their role with respect to other institutions.[33]

In a 1995 study commissioned by the foreign ministries of Sweden, Norway, Denmark, and Finland, a former World Bank senior official concluded that

> MDB shareholders, and particularly the OECD shareholders who are involved in virtually every MDB, need to take a more systematic overall view of the official multilateral financing system.... They need to ask themselves more fundamental questions about where the system as a whole is going, whether it is continuing to perform useful developmental and resource intermediation functions, and how it should be made to change in keeping with new shifts in global capital markets.[34]

Similarly, the former head of the IFC, as well as the British aid agency, wrote:

> A long stretch of time has passed since the creation of the Fund and [World] Bank. The world has changed out of recognition

> over the past half century, and the purposes for which they were created are no longer fully relevant. If these institutions are to go on serving the world well, they will have to adapt and change.[35]

And in the words of former World Bank chief economist Anne Krueger:

> The United States has lacked a consistent vision of the role of the multilateral institutions. U.S. policy toward them has been reactive, as policymakers perceive a problem. . . and then consider the policy instruments available to them. The World Bank, IMF, and regional institutions have been among the instruments to which policymakers have turned, but they have done so only on an ad hoc, case by case basis. Without clearly defined missions, the multilaterals are subject to fickle political currents in the United States and other major shareholders.[36]

Major issues regarding the MDBs that many believe need to be seriously addressed by U.S. policymakers include the following:

- Lessons from recent failures of important MDB programs. The 1998 financial crisis has drawn attention to the large sums the MDBs have lent for "financial sector reform" and "improving the enabling environment for private sector development," only to have the economies of many of their largest recipients suffer near collapse from failings in these areas.
- Implications of shifting private risk to the MDBs. Many proposals have been put forward to expand private flows to developing countries by shifting risk to the MDBs. What are implications for the institutions and their shareholders?
- The MDBs' role with respect to the IMF. What is the appropriate division of labor between the World Bank and the IMF? Should the two institutions be merged?
- The MDBs' role in financial bailouts. The *Washington Post* has written that the World Bank is starting to look like the "cash machine" for international bailouts.[37] What should be the role of the MDBs in short-term liquidity crises?
- Effectiveness of poverty reduction programs. The MDBs have undertaken many activities in the name of poverty reduction, many of which, by the banks' own accounts, have not produced lasting benefits. What approach should the MDBs follow now?

What should be the MDBs' role compared with that of nongovernmental organizations, UN agencies, and bilateral aid programs?

• Use of MDB funds to indirectly subsidize the poor use of the borrower's own resources. The explosions of nuclear devices by India and Pakistan, two of the MDBs' largest borrowers, highlight this problem.

The need for a strategic vision also has arisen frequently regarding regional MDBs. The Canadian North-South Institute's recent volume on the Inter-American Development Bank states: "The assistance already provided to the development of the region also needs to be matched with a comprehensive, compelling, and coherent development strategy."[38] American officials in the IDB report that the institution has made several attempts in the past few years to formulate a strategy for its future role in the hemisphere, attempts that have been hindered by the lack of relevant input by the United States, which was described by one as "not in the game."[39] And two recent studies make note of perceptions in Asia that the United States lacked interest in the Asian Development Bank except for short-term foreign policy issues.[40]

This concern that the United States address major strategic issues on the MDBs led the U.S. executive director at the IDB to write in 1997: "Given these interests of the United States [in the MDBs] and the exigencies of the moment, the time has arrived for U.S. policymakers to explore, in depth, their own mechanisms for setting policy to make more effective use of the MDBs."[41]

Policy Coordination and Dispute Resolution. A striking characteristic of the executive branch policy process on MDBs is the limited circle of decisionmakers, as well as the lack of linkages to decisions on related programs. For at least the past 10 years, most decisions on U.S. MDB policy have been made by a small circle of senior Treasury Department officials without much involvement by officials in other executive branch entities. A few U.S. executive directors at the MDBs have been a significant part of the process, but most have not been included in the inner circle of decisionmakers. On a few political issues, senior State Department officials have had a strong influence.

Over the years a number of mechanisms have been established to try to bring together the views of a broader group of executive branch agencies on MDB policy. In the institutions' early years, a legislatively established National Advisory Council on International Monetary and Financial Policies (NAC), chaired by the secretary of the Treasury, played this role. The role of the NAC member agencies—the State Department, the Commerce Department, the Federal Reserve Board, the Export-Import Bank, and the Office of the Special Trade Representative—was solely to advise the secretary of the Treasury. Therefore, in this era only the most powerful members challenged strongly held Treasury positions. The U.S. bilateral aid agency was not a member of the NAC at this time, nor was the part of the State Department that oversaw U.S. participation in UN aid agencies included in the deliberations of the NAC.

The Carter administration in the late 1970s attempted to more closely coordinate the different types of U.S. transfer programs to developing countries. It established a Development Coordination Committee (DCC) with a slightly different membership (State, AID, Treasury, Commerce, Labor, Agriculture, OMB, the Overseas Private Investment Corporation, NSC, the United States Trade Representative's Office, and Action) and named the head of the U.S. bilateral aid agency (AID) as the DCC chairman. Under DCC's auspices, a Subcommittee on Multilateral Aid was supposed to be chaired by a senior Treasury Department official. This structure barely had been established when the Carter administration, prodded by Congress, established the International Development Cooperation Agency, previously discussed. This organization had just begun work when President Carter was defeated in the 1980 election.

The Reagan administration did not abolish the DCC or IDCA authorities but did not use either structure. Nor did it use the NAC extensively as a coordination vehicle. Instead, the Reagan Treasury performed most coordination functions on the MDBs through the Senior Inter-agency Group for International Economic Policy (SIG-IEP). This new group was chaired by Treasury, and when it infrequently considered MDB issues, those considered usually were related to the ongoing debt crisis or to country-specific concerns. Since that time, interagency coordination on MDBs has been largely ad hoc, but no matter what nomenclature has been used for sporadic meetings, it primarily has served to endorse decisions that have already been made by Treasury officials. Recent reports indicate that at least at intermediate and staff levels the involvement of other agencies in MDB policymaking has decreased further in the last few years, and U.S. negotiating teams for MDB replenishment meetings no longer include State Department or AID members.

In recent years there has not been a serious effort to look at all U.S. transfers to developing countries to devise a strong and coherent rationale, to establish priorities, or to assess the relative performance of the various aid channels. Currently, when the foreign affairs budget is prepared, OMB and, to a lesser degree, the State Department's budget office pull together budget numbers for the various programs and assemble language justifying each part of the budget. This supporting language is checked for consistency of general themes. However, the exercise primarily serves to justify decisions that already have been made by the agencies in charge of individual programs. Conflicts among agency budget aggregates—how much to allocate to MDBs, compared with UN agencies, or various types of bilateral transfers—are usually resolved on the basis of short-term political considerations, such as perceived congressional preferences, or are determined by the relative clout of various cabinet departments.

Currently no part of the executive branch does significant analysis on the overall role of foreign transfers in U.S. foreign economic policy or examines in depth which programs address the highest priority needs or have the best track record. For example, when senior Treasury officials decide, with OMB's concurrence, how much funding the United States will provide to a financial replenishment of the Asian Development Fund, this decision is not related to plans for U.S. bilateral aid to Asia, to what UN agencies are doing in Asia, or to the Export-Import Bank's plans for Asia.

The reason for the lack of comprehensive coordination among the channels of U.S. foreign aid seems to be a deep-seated reluctance by the entities responsible for different aspects to expand the decisionmaking group for their program. No administration in recent years has made the effort to override the individual agencies' preferences to manage their own programs without strong linkages to related activities. One policy-level official in a related department in the Bush administration recalled that although Treasury was not overly anxious to consult anyone on MDB policy, AID was even less interested in taking the views of other agencies into account on its programs.[42]

Congressional Research Service analysts summarized the situation regarding U.S. government interagency coordination of foreign aid:

> Foreign assistance programs are administered by five major U.S. government departments and an assortment of other independent agencies and foundations. . . . Central coordination of these efforts frequently has been regarded as weak and ineffective, with "turf" and jurisdictional considerations getting in the way of efficient program and policy management. . . .[43]

Meanwhile, the files of a number of agencies are littered with the paper trail of either failed coordination initiatives or stiff interagency disputes, as various agencies tried, usually unsuccessfully, to carve out a substantive role on MDB policymaking, only to be thwarted by Treasury's political clout in successive administrations.

Although the inner circle of decisionmakers on MDB issues is small, the ad hoc nature of the decisionmaking process means there are few mechanisms to force the systematic resolution of the disagreements that do arise within this small group. This situation can give rise to various problems.

One possible outcome is rapidly changing decisions on the same issue, such as may take place when the loser in a policy dispute calls more powerful reinforcements into the decision process. This occurred in the case of the IFC capital increase negotiations in the early 1990s when the U.S. position changed significantly several times in the negotiations as additional actors got involved in the dispute.

Another outcome that sometimes occurs, especially in disputes between executive directors and Treasury officials is that each pursues his own preferred policy option to the confusion of other shareholders and MDB managements. This occurred for a time in both the African and Asian banks in the 1980s as U.S. executive directors took far more supportive stances on plans for new private sector affiliates than did Treasury.

When faced with tough choices among alternatives, a third possible outcome is failure to make any decision for a prolonged period. This often takes the form of U.S. support for all-inclusive compromise language, instead of making choices when needed. This may lead to U.S. guidance to the MDBs to pursue either contradictory objectives or more objectives than the institutions can hope to accomplish. American University law professor Jerome Levinson believes that current U.S. policy toward the MDBs is fraught with contradictions that the U.S. policy process is unable or unwilling to resolve, especially between the objective of support for poverty reduction and a sometimes conflicting desire to do all possible to foster the mobility and security of international capital.[44]

In her history of U.S. relations with the World Bank, Catherine Gwin noted:

> At the same time, the United States, along with other countries, has pushed the Bank, especially in recent years, into more and more areas of activity without adequate assessment of existing institutional strengths and weaknesses and without sufficient questioning of how far the institutional capabilities could be stretched. This has caused a serious deterioration in the quality of the Bank's operations.[45]

In international negotiations on future MDB operations, the United States sometimes has been accused of advancing a virtual "laundry list" of things it wants a multilateral bank to do without regard for whether the items on the list are consistent with each other or with the institution's existing mandate. However, each was supported by someone of influence, and no decision on priorities was made.

Policy Implementation. The way the United States seeks to implement its MDB policy is affected by the nature of the policy development process. Because U.S. policies usually develop in reaction to events and decisions may not occur until absolutely required, the United States often is not able to have a dialogue with other MDB members before announcing its policy choices. This process leads to what many have found to be an unnecessarily confrontational U.S. style of operating in the MDBs. U.S. perspectives may not differ much from those of other MDB members, but a U.S. announcement of a detailed position without behind-the-scenes consultations leaves other members with the choice of appearing to acquiesce to a U.S. fiat or of opposing a U.S. policy that may vary only in minor points from a position they could support.

At various times the United States has developed good communication structures with selected other MDB members. During the

Carter administration in the 1970s and the latter part of the Reagan administration in the mid-1980s, U.S. Treasury policymakers devoted a good deal of attention to developing a strong Group of 7 structure on MDBs at both the deputy assistant secretary and more senior levels.[46] (Some types of G-7 meetings have discussed MDB issues in all recent administrations, but they have varied greatly in utility and vitality.) At times, the United States has had strong ties to key Latin American finance ministry officials that have been useful in dealing with problems at the IDB. Also, various MDB executive directors have developed their own coordination networks with some of their counterparts that have worked very well. However, it appears that the attention given to these communications structures waxes and wanes according to the personal inclinations of key officials.

The frequent lack of clear priorities among U.S. objectives also affects U.S. policy implementation. This absence of agreed priorities makes it hard for U.S. officials to strike deals with foreign officials.

Another area where U.S. policy implementation reflects the characteristics of the overall U.S. policy process is in the U.S. inability to provide adequate follow-up to many of its MDB initiatives. The thinly staffed unit following MDBs often lacks the time and the expertise to check on whether the MDBs are taking the actions that have been agreed upon. It is not unusual for the United States to demand in an MDB replenishment negotiation for the institution to produce a new kind of report and then not have time to examine the resulting documents.

For years the United States has given only the most cursory attention to the large quantity of documents produced by the MDBs' evaluation systems. In "portfolio reviews" done by all the banks except the new EBRD in 1992–1994, U.S. policymakers were then surprised to find that the evaluation systems in the IDB and the AfDB were inadequate for the review team to know what portion of projects met their objectives, while the reviews in the World Bank and Asian Development Bank found that a relatively large portion of projects were experiencing problems or were judged to have had unsatisfactory results.[47]

The erratic U.S. follow-up of the policies it propounds appears often to confuse MDB managements and leads to cynicism about whether their adherence to their commitments will be tracked. One senior official in an MDB opined that U.S. policy toward the MDBs would be much improved by giving each bank a list of five priorities the United States really cares about and checking progress on them rigorously each month.[48]

U.S. Appointments to Senior Positions in the MDBs. One of the most important aspects of U.S. policymaking on MDBs is how the United States uses its ability to select and influence the selection of senior MDB leadership. The United States has repeatedly found that if the most senior leadership of an MDB is good and shares U.S. objectives, ways can be found to address many problems. On the other hand, if an institution's most senior leadership is weak or is following a significantly different agenda, the United States, even if it does everything right in its own policymaking, may not be able to maintain a productive relationship. Therefore, how the United States uses its ability to influence decisions on MDB leadership is absolutely critical.

For the most senior MDB positions, a number of informal understandings among major shareholders still guide the selection process. In the World Bank it is accepted that the United States will nominate the president of the bank, with the traditional quid pro quo that the managing director of the IMF will be a European. Few other jobs in the World Bank Group are earmarked for nationals of specific countries or regions, although thus far the head of MIGA has always been Japanese.

In the Inter-American Development Bank, it has been agreed since the bank's inception that the president would be from Latin America and the executive vice president from the United States. Thus far the general counsel and the financial manager also have always been from the United States.

By tradition, the president of the Asian Development Bank is nominated by Japan. The United States holds one of three vice presidencies, but the portfolio of the U.S. vice president has been sharply contested at times. The general counsel of the ADB also is usually an American.

In the African Development Bank, where it is clearly established that the president must be from Africa, no other positions are earmarked for nationals from specific countries. Non-Africans have held few senior positions.

In the EBRD, it was always accepted that the president would be a European, but, after hard bargaining, the United States won the right to nominate the vice president.

In the case of MDB leadership jobs, the country with the right to nominate a candidate almost always consults with other important shareholders informally before making a nomination. In some banks, especially the African Development Bank, rival candidates may be nominated, and the United States has a role in the electoral jockeying that determines the winner. Therefore, in addition to the positions for which the United States can select a candidate, the United States also has input into deciding which candidates are selected for other key positions. Because this informal system of allocating MDB jobs is constantly subject to renegotiation, the United States often has to take a stand on proposed modifications.

Decisions on MDB leadership positions are often difficult. Ideally, senior positions would go to the most able candidate without regard to nationality. However, the tradition of allocating at least a few jobs in each bank on the basis of nationality is strong. The United States, which by tradition controls the greatest number of senior positions, is often under pressure to reduce the number of senior positions it holds, especially when new members join an organization or when U.S. financial contributions decline. In those circumstances, the United States must try to balance the benefits of giving up a position in terms of perceived fairness, with the downside of appearing to be either in a weaker position in a given bank or less interested in it.

When U.S. allies propose candidates about which the United States has doubts, the United States faces a difficult choice. However, experience has shown that raising questions at an early stage and taking the time to check thoroughly on the candidate's background is likely to be much preferable to endorsing a problematic candidate.

It is when the United States has the opportunity to put forward a candidate for a senior MDB position that it has the greatest opportunity to make a favorable impact. Selection of an individual with both appropriate substantive skills and the necessary experience and personal qualities can do much to improve the performance of a multilateral institution.

The candidate the United States selects also is important because of the signal it sends to the institution's management and other shareholders. When it selects an obviously qualified, well-respected candidate, the United States sends a strong message that it thinks the institution is important and is willing to do its part to keep it functioning well. A track record of selecting respected nominees for MDB jobs makes it more likely that other U.S. efforts to improve the institutions' performance will be taken seriously. Also, in some cases the type individual the United States selects sends a message about the U.S. view of the institution's role—for example, the selection of a senior banker signals that the United States sees the institution's role as financial, while the selection of a noted economist or ecologist would send a different message.

Unfortunately, if the United States selects a candidate who does not appear to have appropriate substantive qualifications and experience or who has the wrong personal qualities for the job, this also has a major impact. Not only does the institution's management suffer, so does the credibility of the United States as a shareholder who cares about institutional performance. If the candidates the United States puts forward are perceived to be unqualified, it can negate many other positive policy initiatives because other shareholders will not believe the United States is serious about improving the institution.

Like many other aspects of the U.S. policy process, there is no organized system for selecting U.S. appointees to MDB jobs, and, as is the case for other issues, the decisionmaking loop is usually small. The exception is selection of a nominee for the presidency of the World Bank. Because this position is so visible and widely sought, usually the selection process receives cabinet-level, even presidential, attention. Although some have criticized the U.S. nominees, the job of World Bank president requires an extraordinary mix of qualities, and none of the U.S. selections have appeared to lack serious qualifications for the job.[49]

The U.S. selection process for less prominent jobs has worked far less well. For lower-level positions, the process of selecting candidates usually is ad hoc, depending on the personal preferences of a few senior Treasury officials. At times the U.S. executive director plays an important role, but at times does not. Political-level officials in other U.S. agencies are usually not involved, and often have been sharply rebuffed if they sought to be. By all accounts, Congress—even key members of the administration's own party—are not consulted.[50] At times the executive branch has earned lasting congressional ill will by appearing to remove U.S. officials from MDB jobs for political reasons or by selecting candidates perceived to be unqualified.[51]

Although the United States has put forward several candidates in regional banks that were criticized as lacking appropriate substantive expertise and senior-level experience, the messiest case involved the desire of a few senior U.S. officials to appoint a former mid-level career Treasury official as the ADB's U.S. vice president. This incident came at a time in the late 1980s when ADB management had received extensive press criticism for poor lending practices. The United States had been objecting also to the ADB's zeal to push for a high loan volume even if lending went to countries with questionable policies or for poor projects. The opportunity to nominate a new U.S. vice president appeared to present an excellent opportunity to inject needed high-quality vision into the ADB's management team and send a signal that the United States expected major improvements in the quality of ADB operations.

Instead, after limited internal consultations, the United States put forward the name of the Treasury official. This nomination was received badly by almost everyone at the bank, because the nominee was viewed to lack the senior-level or managerial experience needed for the position. It was widely rumored that he had been interested in, but not selected for, much lower level positions in the bank. The president of the bank repeatedly asked the United States for the names of additional candidates, and at one point a poll of the executive board went heavily against the U.S. nominee. The United States was approached bilaterally by a variety of countries, including Canada, the United Kingdom, and Germany, about the unsuitability of its nominee.[52] Nevertheless, the United States persisted in refusing to nominate other candidates, and the matter remained in an uneasy stalemate for months. Finally, after repeated pressure from the United States, the Japanese Finance Ministry prevailed upon the Japanese president of the ADB to back down and appoint the U.S. candidate.[53] This episode seriously tarnished U.S. relations with a new ADB president and for a substantial period undercut U.S. arguments for improvements in the ADB's performance.

In a number of other cases, capricious decisions on leadership appointments seemed to work against long-term U.S. interests in the MDBs. On one occasion, for unclear reasons the United States blocked the appointment of a long-time senior World Bank official to head the IFC. The official went on to become his country's prime minister and instituted a number of widely hailed economic reforms.

In other circumstances, the United States has ceded important MDB jobs, not because of any thoughtful calculation that this was in the U.S. or the institution's best interest, but simply because the small cadre of Treasury decisionmakers apparently were not acquainted with anyone suitable for the job and were unwilling to cast a broader net for candidates.[54]

Consideration of the history of U.S. appointments in the MDBs implies that the lack of an established process and the small closed circle of decisionmakers for all but the most visible job of World Bank president have contributed to apparently arbitrary decisions that have detracted from U.S. efforts to encourage effective MDB operations.

Executive Branch–Congressional Relations

Like the policy process in the executive branch, the basic outlines of the process by which the executive branch relates to Congress have not changed much over the years. The Treasury Department has long had a strategy of trying to confine serious discussions of MDB issues to a few key members and their staffs, relying on them to persuade others. For long periods this strategy worked quite well. Adroit congressional relations efforts succeeded in persuading key committee and subcommittee chairmen of the wisdom of supporting the MDBs, and when these members had strong opinions on an issue, the Treasury generally found a way to accommodate them.

However, this system of keeping MDB policy an "inside game" with a small group of players has always had the downside of being very vulnerable to changes in a few key personnel. It also made the MDBs vulnerable to whatever particular interests or hobby horses these influential insiders might choose to advocate.

Whatever the faults or virtues of an "insider" congressional relations strategy, many with knowledge of changes in congressional operations believe it is less likely to be effective in the future as fewer members of congressional committees routinely support their chairman's views. Likewise, as more public groups lobby their congressional contacts on MDB issues and as the institutions have become more controversial, it becomes harder for a few insiders to deliver enough votes to pass sizable MDB appropriations.

For nearly a decade, legislation has mandated extensive consultations with Congress before the executive branch makes new commitments for MDB funding. This legislation requires consultations "for the purpose of discussing the position of the executive branch and the views of Congress with respect to any international negotiations being held to consider future replenishments or capital expansions." The legislation also specifies that the consultations should take place "(a) not later than 30 days before the initiation of such international negotiations, (b) during the period in which such negotiations are being held, in a frequent and timely manner, and (c) before a session of such negotiations is held at which the United States representatives may agree to such a replenishment or capital expansion."[55]

The drafter of the legislation intended that these consultations take the form of small group discussions between key legislators and executive branch officials. Such discussions have never been held. Instead, the executive branch has had either individual discussions with members or staff or sent "consultation letters" to the required members.[56] Therefore, the intent of generating a dialogue where different congressional perspectives are represented and agreement on priorities thrashed out has never been fulfilled. The seriousness of the consultations themselves has varied according to political developments and the preferences of key individuals. Recently, even the consultation process with key committee chairmen may have faltered. In early October 1998, the chairman of the House Banking subcommittee that oversees MDBs wrote to the Treasury secretary raising fundamental issues with Treasury's policies vis-à-vis the MDBs and the global economic crisis and asking that there be better consultation with Congress. He received a reply from the secretary early in 1999 after his departure from the subcommittee chairmanship.

In the past, members of Congress who were not part of the "insider" game on MDBs found the process considerably harder to influence. When faced with congressional criticism of the MDBs or with desires for changes in MDB policies, the Treasury has often fallen back either on public relations efforts to convince the critic he is mistaken or on largely rhetorical support for the congressional cause. In the second case, the executive branch will often include the issue in a long list of things the United States wants an MDB to do. The executive branch then may go back to Congress and indicate that lack of support from other MDB members prevented adoption of their proposal. In some cases such absence of other donor support may have been due not to intractable opposition but to the lack of zeal with which the United States presented the proposal or the lack of effort made to explain it and persuade other members.

At other times, the MDB may go along with the congressional proposal and issue a public statement along the lines desired. Problems may arise, however, if someone checks carefully on whether the MDB is fulfilling its commitments. Paul Nelson's recent book, *The World Bank and Nongovernmental Organizations,* explains how some World Bank staff have adopted the term "finessing it" to describe how they handle public rhetoric to take account of a myriad of social, environmental, gender, and other considerations for which their management fails to provide resources or the time to address seriously.[57]

American University's Jerome Levinson makes the same point on the issue of workers' rights, alleging that in spite of favorable executive branch rhetoric and legislation, the Treasury has ignored the workers' rights mandate.[58] The same rhetorical acceptance of a congressional initiative but lack of implementation was alleged also in the case of World Bank energy and forestry policies.[59]

This tendency to try to placate Congress, rather than seriously discuss with members the implications for other priorities of new proposals, has resulted in unclear or inconsistent U.S. policies toward MDBs. Many innovations advocated by Congress, such as the introduction of mechanisms to allow project beneficiaries to play a role in project design, in-depth analysis of social impacts, or measures to improve project implementation are likely to lead to increased MDB administrative costs if done seriously and on a broad scale. The executive branch usually has failed to bring this fact to Congress' attention or acknowledge it in their discussions with MDB managements. Indeed, on many occasions the United States has been supporting such congressional initiatives, while at the same time asking for substantial reductions in MDB administrative budgets. This lack of candid dialogue with Congress encourages its members to avoid needed tradeoffs and to increase demands without considering which existing activities should be sacrificed.

The number of instances where the executive branch and the MDBs have made promises that are not being fulfilled, according to "reality checks" in the field,[60] has led to congressional frustration and attempts to draft legislation that would tie the executive branch's hands more tightly. The prevailing attitude seems to be summed up in a recent statement by Mitch McConnell, chairman of the Senate Appropriations Subcommittee on Foreign Operations, in the context of the 1998 debate on funding the IMF: "Treasury only produces reforms and results when Congress requires action in law."[61]

Congressional fiats sometimes have produced useful reforms in the MDBs, such as the creation of inspection panels, adoption of requirements for environmental assessments, and initiation of incremental improvements in the institutions' information disclosure policies. On other occasions, arbitrary congressional requirements, such as requiring U.S. "no" votes on some kinds of MDB projects, have not been very effective.[62] In addition, congressional requirements for numerous special reports take up limited Treasury staff time but often do not produce a serious change in MDB behavior if it is not clear that senior executive branch officials stand behind the congressional intent.

The lack of meaningful dialogue between the executive branch and some members of Congress interested in MDBs, and among holders of various points of view in Congress, has fostered confusion about U.S. priorities. It has also caused sharp swings in U.S. policy as the political fortunes of various groups rise and fall.

The U.S. policy process on MDBs has remained remarkably unchanged as the MDB system itself has mushroomed in size and intricacy, as the system has become the centerpiece of U.S. official transfers to developing countries, and as the debate on the MDBs' future role and performance has become more insistent. The next chapter will look more specifically at the strengths and weaknesses of this process, and chapter 4 will suggest possible improvements.

3

The Current Process: Relic of an Easier Era?

Strengths

The U.S. policy process on MDBs has a number of strengths, many of which are related to the unchanging and consistent character of the process.

The Current Process Clearly Assigns Responsibility

One frequently cited strength of the U.S. policy process is that it clearly establishes which entity in the executive branch of the U.S. government is in charge on MDB issues. Unlike other areas where responsibilities in the executive branch are shared or overlapping, the Treasury Department's primacy on MDBs is undisputed. If the U.S. government does not speak with one voice all the time, the problem is either a difference of opinion between the executive branch and Congress, which is a situation rooted in the U.S. constitutional doctrine of separation of powers, or it is an internal problem at Treasury, which should be amenable to solution by Treasury leadership.

The current structure also facilitates coordination of international financial initiatives with MDB programs—for example, the Brady Plan for developing country debt.

The Current Process Has Effectively Safeguarded the Financial Soundness of the MDBs

Thus far the U.S. policy process on MDBs has had remarkable success in safeguarding the financial soundness of the institutions themselves, a significant achievement. When the first MDBs were founded, the questions of how they were to access capital markets and whether they could acquire and maintain a prime credit rating were not clear. Also, one has only to consider the number of public and private financial institutions that have experienced serious financial problems in the past 50 years to appreciate the significance of maintaining the MDBs' financial health.

The Treasury Department accomplished this both through maintenance of adequate U.S. policies on financial issues in the MDBs but also by consistently using the leverage required to make a wide variety of MDB managers and shareholders adhere to sound financial policies. The tough-mindedness and consistency of purpose needed to achieve this should not be underestimated.

The Current Process Has Consistently Attracted High Quality Leadership and Staff

In view of the discrepancy between the large amounts of money and complex issues involved in U.S. MDB policy and the small number of individuals responsible for it, it is remarkable that the process has worked as well as it has. This is due to the unusually high caliber of both the political leadership that has been selected to manage MDB policy and to a small cadre of dedicated and talented civil servants who in a number of cases have worked on MDB issues for many years.

The MDBs have benefited from the fact that the Treasury is considered one of the most important cabinet agencies and is therefore able to attract the top talent in incoming administrations. Although the most senior Treasury officials may spend little time on MDB issues, the Treasury Department is small and agile enough so that real emergencies in the MDBs can be brought quickly to senior policymakers' attention, and the quality of the contribution is likely to be significant. Also, perhaps because of the importance of the issues they face, senior Treasury officials have appeared to be more consistent in their approach to problems and less inclined to pursue fads or enthusiasms of the moment than have officials in some other parts of the executive branch.

A particular strength of recent MDB policy has been the talented individuals that have been tapped to serve as deputy assistant secretary of the Treasury overseeing MDB policy. Although over the past 15 years these individuals have had varied backgrounds, with experience ranging from banking to the career Foreign Service to congressional staff, they have almost always been especially competent and hardworking. This job is difficult because it requires constantly addressing a wide range of demanding issues without the time or resources for extensive backup work or analysis. The individual in this position usually negotiates for the United States multibillion-dollar MDB replenishments and often interacts with foreign government counterparts who are much more senior in rank in their governments and likely to have longer experience with MDB issues.

U.S. MDB policy also has benefited from a cadre of especially strong Treasury career officers. This group of 20 to 30 individuals rotated in various positions related to MDBs in Treasury and in executive directors' offices for many years. Although a number of them do not have direct experience in developing countries, their strong intellectual capabilities, economics background, and knowledge of how the MDBs work have made an enormous contribution to the U.S. policy process. This group has provided continuity to U.S. MDB policy and has been able to make up with intellectual agility, willingness to work extraordinarily hard, and knowledge of MDB dynamics what they have lacked in time to do research on issues or in knowledge of specific conditions in developing countries.

Weaknesses

The weaknesses of the current policy process on MDBs also result from its unchanged character and lie in the areas where it has not adapted to changed circumstances, to more difficult challenges, and to the lessons of past failures. The U.S. policy process in this area may be just one of a number of areas where the United States has not yet updated its institutional infrastructure to take account of the changes in the global environment since the end of the Cold War.

The Current Process Places Too Heavy a Burden on the Multilateral Institutions

A fundamental problem with the U.S. policy process on MDBs seems to be that several assumptions underlying the current process have proven to be invalid, and the current system places heavier burdens on multilateral institutions than they can bear successfully. Specifically, the assumption is unrealistic that once a multilateral institution is established, its leading members need only exercise light oversight concerning institutional performance. It is especially unrealistic in the current situation where external changes necessitate difficult choices on the future role of the MDBs.

Current and former officials in the institutions themselves frequently make the most compelling case for stronger shareholder and, often, U.S. oversight of the institutions. A senior Canadian official in one of the MDBs put it most graphically: "Unless you have someone in the U.S. Treasury with all the lights turned on, who is able to reach into the institution, the institution is out of control. . . . Leadership is needed."[1]

Multilateral institutions face more difficult hurdles in maintaining accountability to citizens than do national governments. The reason is simple. For a national institution to be accountable to the people who fund it, only one linkage, that between the institution and the country's citizens, needs to work well. However, to hold international institutions like the MDBs accountable to the taxpayers ultimately providing their financial support requires two linkages to work—that between the citizens and their own government and that between the national government and the international institution.

The former U.S. executive director at the World Bank, James Burnham, noted the difficulty of maintaining a close linkage between any single shareholder government and a multilateral institution when he wrote:

> Effective performance by any public agency depends largely upon the incentives and constraints that the agency's sponsors impose on it. . . . If there are a number of significant sponsors with varying interests, effective performance becomes increasingly difficult to measure or even define, and the staff's own agenda becomes increasingly predominant within the constraints imposed by the sponsors.[2]

Paul Nelson, in his research on the World Bank and nongovernmental organizations, concurred with this judgment noting, "Sovereignty of most members, with respect to the World Bank, then, is limited by the weak accountability of staff to the Board and to the nations they represent."[3]

Within multilateral institutions like the MDBs, the interests of both other member governments and the institution's management may differ from U.S. interests and perspectives. Borrowing members of the MDBs may have as their agenda to maximize foreign currency flows from the institutions with as little interference as possible from the institution in terms of policy conditions or constraints on their actions. Still other MDB members have different perspectives than does the United States on the importance of citizen choice and political pluralism as forces for economic growth.

Of probably greater concern than whether the MDBs will march to the drum of another shareholder to the detriment of U.S. interests is the danger that without strong shareholder leadership, the institutions will chart their future courses in the interests of their own bureaucracies. Although it is tempting to envision that multilateral institutions are run by apolitical international civil servants that will put global interests ahead of national or self-interest concerns, and undoubtedly some MDB leaders and staff fit this description, many observers suggest that international bureaucracies are no more or less self-interested than national ones, but respond to a different set of incentives. However, these incentives may not lead them to do what is in the U.S. interest.

The United States, as the largest donor to the MDBs, has a strong interest in seeing that MDB projects achieve their objectives and that the institutions have systems to accurately evaluate whether they do. Likewise, it is strongly in the U.S. taxpayers' interest when activities traditionally funded by the MDBs can now be adequately financed by either private sources or by developing countries themselves. On the other hand, MDB leaders may not have such a strong interest in seeing their programs rigorously evaluated and may view private funding sources as competition. Efforts to graduate economically improving borrowers to reliance on their own and market resources may be seen as an undesirable reduction in demand for the MDBs' products.[4]

Some particular characteristics of MDB bureaucracies probably incline them to behave in ways not always consistent with U.S. objectives. The former Venezuelan executive director at the World Bank describes the situation regarding employee incentives at that bank:

> While the G-7 has a substantial influence in shaping the content of the policies pursued by the Bank, the G-4 effect greatly

> shapes the way these policies are executed. The G-4 is not a grouping of countries. It is the designation of the U.S. visa that non-U.S. citizens on the Bank staff hold as long as they are employed by it. Together with other benefits to which Bank employees are entitled, it creates a critical dependency on the Bank and significantly shapes its internal culture. . . while job retention tactics influence behavior in all organizations, at the Bank, such tactics acquire an importance that overrides all other concerns.[5]

This aspect of the MDBs' culture fosters risk aversion and creates institutional inertia in favor of maintaining the same programs and processes, even when external circumstances have changed or when doubts exist about whether the programs are working. Another former World Bank senior official concluded a 1995 study as follows: "At the very least, some effort needs to be made for annual reviews, through an appropriately constituted body, of how the MDB system is performing. . . . Left to their own devices, and their self-absorbed managements, there is a serious risk that the MDBs will, before too long, atrophy as constructive institutional forces in promoting the cause of development."[6]

MDB managements may use their leverage as dispensers of large loans to developing country governments to pressure the executive directors from borrowing countries not to join donor country directors in supporting reforms in the institutions. Former U.S. executive directors at both the World Bank and the IDB noted that executive directors from developing countries sympathetic to U.S. reform objectives often had obvious difficulties in supporting U.S. initiatives that were opposed by the institutions' managements.[7]

In the face of these potential differences in interests between MDB managements and shareholders, the United States has remained passively content to accept uncritically a succession of changing MDB management strategies to try to address a barrage of bad news about MDB performance in the past 5 to 10 years. Both the evaluation reports from the institutions themselves and many reports from outside groups reveal that most of the MDBs are having serious problems achieving their basic development effectiveness objectives. The 1997–1998 global economic crisis has spotlighted major weaknesses in developing country economies in the very areas where the MDBs have long provided large-scale funding for "reforms" (for example, the financial sector in Indonesia, Russia, Venezuela, and Mexico). The World Bank's own evaluation data have shown for several years that fewer than half the projects evaluated are expected to be able to sustain their benefits after MDB funds have stopped flowing and about one-third fail to meet the bank's tests of development effectiveness.[8]

According to World Bank sources also, the problems are particularly acute in such areas as institutional development, financial reform, and macroeconomic and sectoral reform, the areas where MDB efforts are likely to be most critical in the years ahead. On the other hand, the area in which the MDBs seem to be having the greatest success—meeting physical construction targets—is one in which private funds are most likely to be available in a number of countries. Although pervasive MDB secrecy makes it hard for outside groups to examine the MDBs' work, external studies also have revealed significant problems.[9]

The executive branch response to the various reports of unsuccessful MDB programs at times has been to view them primarily as a public relations problem or as a bottleneck to securing appropriations from Congress. The United States has not conducted its own analyses of the causes of problems or examined in depth the prospects of the successive generations of MDB proposals to fix the problems. Likewise, since the congressionally mandated and relatively modest changes in MDB information policies of 1993, the United States has not effectively expanded the transparency of MDB operations to give U.S. government and nongovernmental groups a better idea of what caused the problems and whether MDB plans to make improvements were on the right track and being implemented.

The Current Process Is Too Closed to Nongovernmental Concerns

A second way in which U.S. policymaking toward the MDBs has not kept pace with changing circumstances is that the process has remained quite closed to most nongovernmental actors. When the MDBs were first established, their role in providing funding to developing countries compared with the role of U.S. bilateral aid was relatively small. Therefore, when Americans wanted to influence their aid programs, they usually lobbied for changes in U.S. bilateral programs. However, now that the MDBs are playing a more important role, it is logical that various U.S. public groups would like to be more involved in how their government develops its policies toward these influential institutions.

Also, when the MDBs were established, fewer Americans were knowledgeable about and interested in developing countries than is the case now. In addition, the ongoing Cold War required a greater degree of secrecy about the international affairs policy process than is needed today.

At this juncture, however, the vast improvements in global transportation and communications have spawned much greater interest in remote areas on the part of many U.S. individuals and groups. An array of civil society organizations—religious, professional, educational, business, labor, cultural, ethnic—now takes an interest in the economic status of developing countries. It has also become increasingly clear that the way the United States exerts influence in the world extends much beyond government policies and actions. The influence of U.S. business, of U.S. educational institutions, and of U.S. charitable organizations may affect developing countries more than most decisions taken by the U.S. government.

In this context it makes sense to ground U.S. policy initiatives toward the MDBs more thoroughly in the perspectives of interested nongovernmental groups. This approach offers the opportunity both to ensure that U.S. MDB policies reflect American values and to give these multilateral institutions greater legitimacy with a broader spectrum of Americans.

The degree of interest that individual Americans take in developing countries can be seen by the contributions they make. Several years ago a report on U.S. foreign aid estimated that individual Americans donated $12 billion to $15 billion a year in time and money to people and causes in the developing world and that private-based religious organizations, nonreligious private voluntary groups, philanthropic foundations, and U.S. universities spend far more than all forms of U.S. government economic assistance combined.[10]

The U.S. business community is also taking a broader interest in the work of the MDBs. In the past, the interests of U.S. business in the MDBs often were limited to a few types of firms and to a few specialized areas of interest. Firms knowledgeable about and seriously interested in the MDBs were primarily heavy equipment suppliers, service vendors (such as consulting engineering firms), and a few large U.S. banks. Their areas of interest primarily were MDB procurement and financial policies. However, with globalization making more U.S. firms dependent on economic conditions around the world, many more U.S. businesses now have a stake in the quality of the policy advice provided by the MDBs and even in whether MDB poverty programs are effective in dampening rural unrest in Mexico or urban discontent in Jakarta. The focus and quality of MDB programs to improve competition policy, enforce labor standards, and regulate financial systems will immediately affect many types of U.S. businesses. They have a substantial stake in the direction and soundness of U.S. policy toward these influential institutions.

Although their efforts have been inconsistent, some of the MDBs have responded to the growing interest and importance of private groups by making increased efforts to reach out and work with selected nongovernmental groups in developed and developing countries.

The U.S. policy process, however, has not changed to become more open to these diverse nongovernmental interests. In general, nongovernmental groups' views are considered only if they have ties to senior Treasury Department officials or are well organized and politically powerful enough to win strong congressional support. Even the groups that have occasionally succeeded in influencing the process are not convinced they can count on being consulted when the issues they care about arise.

The Current Process Fails to Develop Coherent U.S. Strategies for the Major Institutions

Evidence suggests that if the United States really wants something in the World Bank or the IDB, and to a lesser degree in the ADB and the EBRD, it is likely to get it, provided that the United States propounds its position in the right way.[11] This means that the United States makes clear that a particular issue has top priority, that the U.S. government is united in its position, and that the request comes from an appropriate level in the government (cabinet level or above). Also, the United States needs to give the institution time to act and must make its wishes known clearly but discreetly enough so that multilateral decisionmaking processes are not compromised.

The sources of U.S. influence in the MDBs are multiple and sometimes subtle, and this stronger U.S. influence distinguishes MDBs most clearly (in the U.S. perspective) from the UN agencies that also promote international development objectives. First, the MDBs are deliberately not structured to try to give all members equal influence (unlike most UN bodies). Votes in the MDBs are related to financial contributions, which, in turn, are generally related to a member's relative role in the global economy.[12]

Second, the instrumental role of the United States in founding the World Bank, IDB, and ADB continues to give it influence and the right to exercise some special privileges instituted at the banks' inception (veto rights over charter changes in the World Bank and over some lending windows in the IDB, coequal voting rights with Japan in the ADB, and the right to nominate candidates for specified senior-level jobs). Likewise, because the European nations that founded the EBRD were eager for U.S. support for the new bank, the United States was able to negotiate the largest voting share and the right to nominate the vice president.

The third, and perhaps most important, source of U.S. influence in the MDBs is overall economic, financial, political, and military strength. The United States derives much influence in the MDBs, as in other international organizations, from its position as the last superpower—leverage that can be expected to wax and wane with general perceptions of U.S. strength and resolve. Additional leverage is received from the MDBs' need to secure U.S. approval to borrow U.S. currency in capital markets.

Finally, U.S. influence in the MDBs is related to its current financial support for them.[13] This relationship is probably not as simple or as short term as successive administrations have tried to paint it to reluctant congressional appropriators. The United States has been in arrears on negotiated contributions to some MDBs for most of their history, and U.S. influence has not plummeted. Likewise, withholding contributions in some cases can enhance U.S. influence. This was the case in the IDB, where U.S. refusal to agree to a funding replenishment in the mid-1980s until other members agreed to change some aspects of IDB operations enhanced U.S. influence and decreased the ability of influential borrowing governments to obtain large loans for questionable purposes.[14]

Nevertheless, if the United States is perceived as having permanently decided to back away from funding the MDBs for reasons beyond the control of the institution or the other shareholders (that is, for U.S. budget reasons rather than poor institutional performance), one of two things would happen. Either other donors would also back away from the institution and the bank's importance would decline, or other important donors would take the U.S. place, however reluctantly, in financing the institution and also in exerting influence in it.

U.S. influence in all of the MDBs, except perhaps the African Development Bank, is potentially very large, yet successive administrations have repeatedly told Congress and the public that it had been unable to secure adoption of this or that proposed policy change. Therefore, the explanation must lie in how the United States uses its influence. How the United States marshals and expends its leverage in the MDBs is closely related to the lack of strategic focus in the policy process.

The United States does not regularly or systematically consider whether each MDB is still needed from the U.S. perspective and, if so, what its most important functions are. Nor does it consider whether these functions are being performed well, whether there are problems, and, if so, what changes are needed.[15] Careful consideration of these questions would determine whether the United States should devote substantial attention to the institution and lay the basis for decisions about which issues are more important than others for the United States.

In cases where a strategy formation process reveals differences of opinion, it is especially important that they be resolved clearly. Apparently the lack of effective U.S. policy on important MDB issues often stems from disagreements that key players are reluctant to acknowledge or press to resolution. Therefore, the United States either advocates so many priorities it is ineffective or advocates positions so inconsistently it does not achieve results.

The current ad hoc, informal policy and dispute resolution process is inadequate to resolve the inevitable disagreements. A more structured process is needed that clearly articulates the various points of view, who supports them and why, and then lays the issue before a higher authority for resolution.

A strategy formulation process for each MDB that results in clear choices among alternatives would provide numerous advantages. The process itself would highlight gaps in information or analysis, such as the lack of credible information on institutional performance. The resulting strategy would guide all U.S. players, allowing MDB issues of less importance to be downplayed while freeing staff time and permitting U.S. priorities to be tracked carefully. A clear U.S. strategy would permit U.S. officials negotiating with other shareholders to "trade off" issues of lower priority to achieve agreement on things of greater importance to the United States. MDB leaders would better understand how the United States judges their performance. Finally, if political fortunes changed, the strategy would inform the new regime about the judgments of the previous administration and the reasons for them.

The U.S. Policy Process toward MDBs Is Not Sufficiently Linked to Policies on Related Issues

In the executive branch the process of formulating MDB policy is divorced from many other aspects of U.S. policy toward developing countries. In fact, U.S. policy toward developing countries, including U.S. policy on its various types of financial transfers to the developing world, is formulated by a bewildering hodge-podge of cabinet departments and agencies.

Lack of Coordination of U.S. Economic Policies toward Developing Countries. Since the experiment with the IDCA structure in the 1970s, there have been few comprehensive attempts to more closely integrate the various U.S. policies that affect developing countries. Efforts that have been made have usually been initiatives to deal with particular regions or crisis situations—for example, transition in Russia and Eastern Europe.

Congressman Lee Hamilton described the situation in 1988, and evidence suggests that little has changed:

> There is no regular programmatic/policy level coordination and integration of U.S. policies and programs toward developing countries. There is a systematized annual budget process, but the various pieces are brought in separately by the individual agencies. The pieces are reviewed as a whole by OMB, but that review is principally from a budget perspective. To the extent there is integration/coordination, it occurs at the field level, within a country mission by a strong ambassador. There needs to be a single point in the U.S. foreign economic policy establishment which brings together the various instruments of U.S. policy—trade, investment, debt, food assistance and sales, economic and security assistance, science and technology, environment, etc.[16]

This fragmentation of U.S. economic policy toward developing countries sometimes results in U.S. policies working at cross-purposes. The most striking examples are generally cases where U.S. trade or investment policy works at cross-purposes with U.S. foreign assistance.

It has long been known that developing countries' economic situations are affected much more strongly by changes in trade policies than they are by the smaller resources foreign aid donors can muster. A report of the UN Development Program stated that trade restrictions reportedly cost the developing countries $500 billion a year, 10 times what they receive in foreign assistance.[17] Although it is possible to dispute the statistics, there is little doubt that factors affecting trade flows matter more to developing countries than does foreign aid.

On occasion, these aspects of U.S. economic policy do work at cross-purposes. An often-cited example concerns Bangladesh, one of the world's poorest countries and traditionally one of the biggest recipients of donor aid. In Bangladesh, U.S. officials urged the government to promote manufactured exports of labor-intensive goods. Bangladesh changed its policies, and soon clothing exports soared in response. Shortly thereafter, U.S. trade officials pressured the government of Bangladesh into accepting quotas that would restrict their apparel exports to the United States, and these restrictions have continued.[18]

Also, as table 1-4 in chapter 1 noted, foreign private investment now outstrips official development finance by a significant margin, and changes in U.S. regulations and laws affecting foreign investment can have a very significant effect, either positive or negative, on developing countries. The range of investment policy or regulatory changes that are important has increased with the growth in the importance of portfolio investment in developing countries, in addition to the more traditional direct investment.

Although the conflict between U.S. aid and trade or investment policy toward developing countries often has been harmful, it is easy to see the cause of the problem. The United States, like most countries, has strong domestic interests affected by trade and investment policy decisions. It never will be easy to reconcile specific harms to domestic groups with efforts to assist developing countries. However, the problems flowing from the lack of coordination among the bureaucracies that oversee the various types of U.S. transfers to developing countries are harder to justify.

Lack of Coordination of U.S. Transfers to Developing Countries. An analysis by the President's Commission on the Management of AID Programs stated at the end of 1992 that "the number of Executive Branch agencies involved in foreign assistance is growing. Senior-level coordination is weak. The Executive Branch runs a real danger of losing control over the priorities and roles of various agencies in foreign assistance and the allocation of funds."[19]

Michael O'Hanlon of the Brookings Institution contrasts the situation of U.S. transfers to developing countries, where funds are provided by a variety of U.S. agencies under weak or nonexistent central coordination, with that of defense policy, where the central policy formulation and coordinating role of the secretary of defense is long established.[20] The fragmentation of U.S. economic aid, even considering only the more significant programs—currently bilateral aid under AID, the MDBs under Treasury, UN aid under State/IO, and food aid overseen by the Department of Agriculture—threatens to worsen because some of the fastest growing programs, such as refugee assistance and counternarcotics programs, are overseen by yet a different bureaucratic entity (the State Department's Global Affairs Bureau).[21] It is not yet clear what will be the practical effect of recent legislation formalizing the reporting relationship of the head of AID to the secretary of state. This will depend on arrangements to implement the change as well as any efforts that might be made to improve internal State Department coordination on foreign transfers.

This fragmentation of U.S. programs to provide resources to developing countries, unlike the lack of coordination between U.S. aid and trade policy, is not driven by the existence of important divergent U.S. interests. Rather, it appears to stem from the desire of the various bureaucracies for programmatic autonomy. However, the fragmentation is taking a toll in a variety of ways on the U.S. ability to effectively assist developing countries. Because U.S. foreign assistance programs are no longer protected by their Cold War security rationale, their successes and failures have become more open to scrutiny, and the problems stemming from fragmentation loom larger.

One consequence of the fragmentation of U.S. foreign assistance is that it reduces the chances for the formulation of a well-constructed and clearly articulated intellectual framework for foreign transfers that can be analyzed and debated. In the absence of an overall executive branch analytical framework for aid, the proponents of individual programs have relied on loose generalizations and weak causality linkages that fail to satisfy even mild skeptics.

Developing a sound analytical framework for official transfers in an era when private resources are much more readily available to countries pursuing good policies requires grappling with difficult issues. These include examining the linkage between the resources to be provided and the desired outcome—that is, how and under what conditions U.S. funding will strengthen civil society in Bosnia or accelerate economic growth in Africa. It also includes specifying the reason external resources (usually only a tiny portion of a recipient country's budget) are needed—that is, why the country could not fund the program itself if it accorded the activity high priority. The need for more rigorous analysis to justify aid expenditures was made compellingly by the World Bank itself when it noted:

> The evidence. . . is that aid is often fungible, so that what you see is not what you get. . . . Thus even rigorous project selection or reallocation of donor finance to laudable activities cannot guarantee the effectiveness of aid in a distorted environment. To measure the effect of their finance donors must look at overall allocations and, even more important, at the efficacy of public spending.[22]

The loose causality linkages and weak argumentation advanced to support some U.S. aid programs are especially harmful in the face of widespread perceptions, whether correct or not, that many previous aid efforts have not produced good results. These concerns are advanced in the media even by aid supporters. As former World Bank senior vice president William Ryrie wrote in 1995:

> Overall, the international agencies do not appear to have had a strong positive impact on the policies followed in the large Asian and Latin American economies. . . . Sub-Saharan Africa has not suffered from lack of attention from donors. . . . the overall picture is one of large and rising volumes of aid combined with falling standards of living, failure by the basic test of development.[23]

The uncertainties and difficulties of supporting economic development argue for the executive branch to make better efforts to present a well-thought-out and credible case for its proposed programs. The current widespread fragmentation of aid programs, however, makes it hard to determine the overall rationale for U.S. foreign transfers or to gauge whether U.S. initiatives have a reasonable chance of success. As long as these programs are scattered throughout the executive branch with weak substantive coordination, a strong and carefully analyzed justification may well not be made. The programs will remain vulnerable, not only to the ideological opponents of aid, but also to those in the public at large and in the foreign policy community who may be sympathetic to the purposes of foreign transfers but skeptical about results.

If fragmentation of aid programs in the executive branch causes problems in making a persuasive case for their approval, it causes even worse problems in trying to ascertain the results of the various programs and use analysis of program performance to guide decisions on future U.S. funding.

Currently, some programs funded by the United States do not produce credible evaluation results (for example, some UN agencies); the evaluation material of some programs are reviewed so cursorily within the U.S. government that serious judgments about its quality and implications are often not made (for example, the MDBs); and the evaluation results of other programs (for example, some bilateral programs) have long been questioned by outside observers. Most problematic, the bureaucratic entity knowledgeable about each of the programs primarily serves as its advocate in budget formulation, so little effort is made in the executive branch to systematically and impartially judge program results and allocate future funding to the most effective programs.

OMB budget analysts have long and strenuously pressed for better evaluation data on many of the aid programs, but often have not succeeded in getting it. OMB also does not have the staff to review in detail the evaluation data of the various transfer programs and must rely on the individual agencies for most analysis of whatever performance information is available.

A number of previous examinations of U.S. foreign assistance have decried the lack of performance data on the various programs and called for better evaluation efforts. The Carlucci Commission in 1983 listed improving evaluation as one of its major recommendations, saying: "We recommend the development of a comprehensive evaluative mechanism that assesses the secondary as well as primary impacts of U.S. mutual assistance efforts, interrelates the projects and expresses a judgment on their effectiveness." This commission also recommended independent U.S. evaluations of MDB and UN programs.[24]

In late 1992 the President's Commission on the Management of AID Programs concluded:

> In fiscal year 1992, the U.S. government spent $14.2 billion on foreign assistance programs. However, funding for the nineteen executive branch agencies involved in foreign assistance is not made on the basis of an explicit government-wide strategy or set of priorities. Without an overall rationale and guidance, it is not clear whether foreign assistance resources are being channeled effectively.[25]

It is never easy to establish even-handed evaluation mechanisms for complex programs and allocate funding to some extent on comparative results, but the current fragmented U.S. foreign assistance system makes such allocation almost impossible.

In a third area where program fragmentation hurts U.S. foreign assistance efforts, various programs supported by the United States may work at cross-purposes, or, at a minimum, opportunities for synergism are missed. On many occasions, the policies of some of the multilateral aid entities, to which the United States often was the largest donor, have been at variance in key areas with policies of the U.S. bilateral aid program. Issues that inspired major differences between the U.S. bilateral program and the MDBs for substantial periods include the role of the private sector, emphasis on primary health care, the importance of population programs, use of especially created units outside regular ministries to manage projects, requirements for unsubsidized interest rates in on-lending programs, and a variety of environmental matters.

In some of these cases, the position of the United States in the MDB governing bodies, as determined by the Treasury Department, was to support the USAID position; in other cases the U.S. representative supported the MDB view. In a few cases, USAID and various MDBs have jointly funded projects that the U.S. MDB director opposed in the bank's executive board.

The lack of an effective coordination mechanism for foreign transfer programs in the U.S. government has led the officials in charge of the various U.S. programs to see no need to tailor their approaches to be consistent with those of the other U.S.-supported programs. USAID seldom sought or adhered to the views of the Treasury Department or U.S. executive directors of the MDBs, even on financial issues. Similarly, Treasury did not necessarily follow the advice of USAID, even on development issues. The Treasury Department and the State Department's Bureau of International Organization Affairs, or IO, rarely communicated about the substance of UN and MDB aid programs or about U.S. policy thrusts toward them.[26]

Efforts by any U.S. agency to marshal the support of the rest—for example, efforts by USAID to get Treasury and IO to urge the MDBs and UN agencies to take a different position on an issue—normally encountered such high "transaction costs" in explaining the problem and persuading the others to adopt a common position, it was only attempted for the highest priority and most urgent issues. For more routine business, attempts to get U.S. aid efforts to reinforce each other often were not initiated because of bureaucratic obstacles.

This lack of ability of the various aid spigots to work together in addressing problems led the Carlucci Commission to conclude: "The present program is procedurally and organizationally fragmented. It needs a comprehensive, analytical and institutionalized approach to problem solving."[27]

If fragmentation of U.S. foreign assistance leads to less well-justified programs that are not necessarily funded on the basis of performance and may be working at cross-purposes with each other, it is not surprising that this system also takes a toll on program credibility and public support. The multiple voices in the executive branch that are advocating a variety of programs seem designed to cause problems for aid supporters and provide fodder for critics. Fragmentation works against a clear public sense of why foreign aid is needed, what has been achieved, and what the respective role is of the different programs.

Finally, the fragmentation of U.S. aid efforts results in poor use of U.S. personnel resources. In a few cases duplicative expertise is maintained by agencies in charge of the various aid spigots (for example, nearly all agencies claim economic expertise). More commonly, some of the programs, especially the MDBs and, to a lesser degree, UN aid agencies are not overseen by a U.S. entity that has expertise about most of their areas of activity. The lack of coordination among the U.S. aid entities has meant that specialized expertise is shared only in occasional special arrangements that have high "transaction costs."

The U.S. oversight mechanism for the MDBs seems to be particularly disadvantaged in terms of the quantity and range of expertise available. The recent U.S. executive director at the IDB, L. Ronald Scheman, described this problem:

> Given the enormous depth of technical and intellectual resources of the various agencies of the U.S. government, . . . it may be time to re-examine the way that the United States relates to the MDBs. . . . Development programs, if they are to be meaningful, require technical experts to analyze technical issues. The present machinery of the U.S. government applied to dealing with the MDBs does not automatically bring such expertise to bear. The same is true for U.S. objectives in the private sector. . . . A number of . . . U.S. agencies. . . . manage programs related to our national interests in those [private sector] matters. It would be beneficial if these agencies could be more integrated into the decisionmaking machinery.[28]

Over the years, a number of others have come to the same conclusion about the need for greater breadth of expertise to be involved in monitoring the work of the MDBs and developing U.S. policy. The Carlucci Commission noted the need for "greater attention" to be "devoted by the U.S. Government to the developmental aspects of programs and projects conducted by the MDBs."[29] Former IDB executive vice president Ray Sternfeld believes that "Treasury's focus is too narrow," but thinks what is needed is not technical expertise in the variety of program areas funded by the MDBs, but a more sophisticated focus on the management of large and complex organizations, including people who are able to make credible judgments about the functioning of complex development institutions.[30] A senior U.S. official in one of the MDBs believed the United States had missed major opportunities to press his institution to undertake environmentally beneficial programs because those involved in developing U.S. policy lack sufficient substantive expertise in this area.[31] Others believe the United States fails to bring to bear sufficient expertise on issues such as corporate governance and business practices.

The problem is not that the United States does not have adequate expertise in the areas needed. The United States has an agency that is considered a world-wide model for designing environmentally beneficial programs (the Environmental Protection Agency) and others that have pioneered innovative financial mechanisms to spur private investment in developing countries (for example, the Overseas Private Investment Corporation). Likewise, the U.S. government employs a large number of people to provide expertise in the economic, social, and political evolution of developing countries. In fact, currently USAID has about 5,800 people on its payroll (including personal service contractors and foreign nationals), many of whom were hired for expertise in various aspects of development. They administer foreign aid programs worth about $7.1 billion.[32]

USAID obviously requires more personnel in its work of directly administering its programs than does a U.S. agency that is monitoring and overseeing the work of a multilateral institution. Also, it is possible in the future that priority for U.S. funding could shift to require relatively stronger USAID staffing. Nonetheless, the contrast is striking between USAID's staff of 5,800 and the approximately 45 people in the Treasury Department and in the U.S. executive directors' offices that monitor the more than $50 billion spent by the MDBs each year.

The problem of the thinly stretched, somewhat narrow expertise available to U.S. policymakers on the MDBs could be solved by various types of cooperative arrangements among U.S. agencies to share expertise. On occasion, arrangements of this type have been made, although never on a substantial scale involving the MDBs. In an arrangement flowing out of the 1970s IDCA legislation, USAID detailed about 10 development experts to the State Department's Bureau of International Organization Affairs for a number of years. These individuals served in positions of some authority (for example, as director of the bureau's development office). After several years, however, this arrangement fell victim to USAID's desire to cut back on what it believed to be peripheral activities in order to concentrate its expertise on its own programs. USAID withdrew its officer in the U.S. executive director's office at the ADB a few years ago for the same reason.

These decisions illustrate the constraints that limit the impact of ad hoc arrangements to share personnel among U.S. aid agencies. If the agency providing the expertise has no mandate from Congress or the president to share in management of the program and is not given a substantive role in decisionmaking about it, this agency has no lasting motivation to make available valuable expertise. At times, the agency makes available individuals whose skills or work habits make them unsuitable for other positions. When the donating agency faces a budget crunch, the jobs providing help to other agencies are usually the first to be eliminated.

On the other hand, when an agency readily offers high-quality talent to help with another agency's programs, it is often interpreted, sometimes correctly, as an attempt to carve out a more important role in decisionmaking on the program in question. Concern that this was the case motivated the Treasury Department to repeatedly refuse USAID's offers of nonreimbursable assistance in several of the U.S. executive directors' offices in the mid-1980s.

Any effort to make broader expertise available to the policymaking process on MDBs would need to consider whether other types of expertise would be used to meaningfully broaden U.S. policy considerations. If the current lack of concern for more in-depth MDB oversight continues and if Treasury Department personnel remain unconvinced that considerations beyond economic or financial issues are central to decisions on the role and performance of the institutions, then widening the array of available skills may not lead to a broader-gauged policy process.

The Policy Process Lacks Sufficient Candid Dialogue between the Executive Branch and Congress

The U.S. policy process on MDBs would benefit from broader, more systematic, and more candid consultations between the executive branch and Congress. Attempts to continue to play an "inside game" and limit meaningful consultations to a few members and staff in the face of relatively widespread congressional questions about the institutions are not likely to work. If such tactics do succeed in securing MDB funding for a couple of years while members focus on other issues, it could easily be at the price of a more pervasive lack of knowledge of the MDBs in Congress and growing suspicions about their role and performance. These unaddressed concerns could result in worse problems for the institutions with Congress later.[33]

Policy Implementation Requires More Consistency, Planning, and Prioritization

The United States needs to be more consistent in following up on the implementation of its policy initiatives in the MDBs. The development of a more strategic policy formulation process that specifies priorities more clearly would help to achieve this. Also, a more rational allocation of U.S. government personnel that gives the MDB policy process access to resources commensurate with the importance of MDB programs would help.

The United States also needs to make more carefully considered efforts to persuade other MDB members of the soundness of its policy thrusts. After identifying a hierarchy of issues it wishes to pursue, the United States needs to plan more carefully how to develop a coalition of other members to pursue its objectives. Even in cases where the United States has the influence itself to get an MDB to make a policy change, it is much sounder practice to do the extra work to persuade others of the desirability of the action. A recent case in which the United States made a deal with another large shareholder in the Inter-American Development Bank on a series of issues without regard for the views of most other members was seen by many as harmful to constructive relationships in that institution.

One of the strongest themes emerging from interviews with representatives of other member governments and MDB managements was the belief that the United States had often caused itself unnecessary problems by the manner in which it has sought to implement some of its MDB policies. One knowledgeable official in an MDB, who has worked in the U.S. government, said, "This issue is not about the U.S. not getting its way. Instead it's about the manner in which the United States goes about getting its way."[34] One of the authors of the World Bank's authorized history recently noted that the United States lately has appeared to be less "self-restrained" than in the past about openly seeking to exert its will on the World Bank on some issues.[35] Similarly, a senior World Bank official expressed concern that recent blatant and public U.S. efforts to influence Bank policies in the macroeconomic area would hinder the Bank's efficacy with some borrowers.[36]

Many observers think the United States should pay more consistent attention to consultation mechanisms with other shareholders. Although some current and former U.S. officials are viewed as excellent at developing productive relationships with foreign counterparts, this aspect of their role seems heavily dependent on their personal priorities.

On some occasions the style in which the United States has pressed its points has become an issue itself. Professor Dennis

Yasutomo of Smith College draws on long acquaintance with the Japanese Finance Ministry to detail how the Japanese perceived U.S. MDB initiatives in the 1980s: "The way American spokespersons propound these beliefs causes unnecessary contention. The United States said things in a strong, severe way, and thus received retorts from all sides. The problem is not the content per se, but the way of saying things. It was a problem of style. . . . It was a problem of nuances."[37]

One nuance to be considered may be the rank of officials selected to perform certain tasks. For example, in the 1980s the United States assigned a deputy assistant secretary of the Treasury to give a very tough message of U.S. discontent with a president of the ADB to a much more senior official in the Japanese Finance Ministry. The message was not well received, and some believed that a more senior U.S. official would have been given a different response.

As the MDBs grapple with increasingly difficult issues, the United States must consistently work toward creating a coalition that will support its MDB policies at the least political cost to the United States.

4
Recommendations and Conclusions

When making recommendations about changes in policy processes, this study, like others, confronts the question of the importance of organizational structure and processes in relation to both top-level leadership and the quality of personnel occupying key positions. Obviously, all three are essential to the development and implementation of U.S. policies toward the MDBs.

The following recommendations assume presidential leadership to establish a coherent economic and foreign policy framework for U.S. transfers to developing countries and, specifically, U.S. policies toward the MDBs. No improvements in the process of formulating U.S. policy toward MDBs will produce good policies if the administration in office does not provide such a foundation. It is also very useful if the president and his senior advisers personally exercise leadership on U.S. policy toward developing countries and on efforts to ensure that their preferred organizational structure on these issues works well.

Moreover, it is impossible to say enough about the desirability of any administration's selecting good appointees for key positions and a presidential personnel process that appropriately judges which positions require the highest qualifications and which can be allotted to individuals whose credentials are less proven or who need a longer learning period. Any organizational or policy process improvements can be undone by either unqualified personnel or individuals lacking the desire to make the process work.

In some areas, however, changes in the U.S. policy process to take account of changed conditions and the more difficult challenges confronting the MDBs appear likely to improve the chances of getting good results. These recommendations are suggested in the spirit of the conclusion of the "Tower Report" on the National Security Council in the 1980s: "Process will not always produce brilliant ideas, but history suggests it can at least help prevent bad ideas from becoming Presidential policy."[1]

Develop a Clear U.S. Strategy for Each Major Institution

To achieve a clearer strategic focus for the U.S. policy process on the MDBs, the executive branch should look at each multilateral institution of major importance and develop a strategy for U.S. participation in it.[2] This process should first assess the role of the institution. In the U.S. view, is the institution still needed? If so, for what purposes? Which of its functions are more important? How should this institution relate to others performing similar functions?

The second part of the strategy process should assess the performance of the institution. How does the United States define success and failure for this institution? Does the United States have enough information to know if the institution's programs are achieving their objectives? If this information is not available, why is it not, and how can the problem be rectified? If there are problems with institutional performance, how can the United States address them? What will the United States do, over what time frame, if problems are not addressed? How does the performance of this institution compare with that of others?

On the basis of judgments about the institution's role and performance, the strategy should lay out specific plans for future U.S. participation. What issues should take priority over others and why? Are there conflicts among U.S. objectives, and how might these be resolved? Should U.S. resources for the institution be reduced or increased? Should the availability of U.S. resources be contingent on future actions by the institution or other shareholders?

Finally, the strategy should discuss the tactics the United States plans for advising others of U.S. priorities and building a coalition to achieve its objectives at the least political cost to the United States. Because U.S. expenditures for the MDBs should be linked to analysis of their role and performance, these strategies should be prepared in anticipation of major MDB funding replenishments.

This strategy formulation process should involve interested congressional members and their staffs and should be at least partially open to nongovernmental groups and the public. The resulting strategy should be made public (with any portions pertaining to confidential national security interests included in a classified addendum). If significant changes in the electoral landscape bring in new players or alter the balance of power on MDB issues, strategies will need to change. However, if the process has involved members of Congress in a bipartisan way and included the participation of a range of public groups, the strategies and resulting U.S. policies are likely to change less than if U.S. policies had been developed by a closed circle of current administration insiders.

A new administration taking over might wish to begin the strategy process by looking at all foreign aid spigots together or looking at all similar multilateral institutions at once.[3] This would enable a new administration to start from the ground up to determine relative priorities and take account of interrelationships among institutions. In 1981 the new Reagan administration undertook such an in-depth review of U.S. participation in the MDBs, and the result served as a guide for U.S. policy for a number of years.

Once any administration, with input from Congress and public groups, has decided which MDBs and other multilateral institutions it deems most important, it can then individually review those institutions to develop strategies toward each and specifically focus on progress toward objectives.

The process of articulating a U.S. strategy for individual multilateral institutions may help to persuade other members to support U.S. policy choices. A representative of a major MDB shareholder government noted concerns that the United States "needs to follow a more continuous process" toward aid issues and act with greater consistency, rather than adopting a series of "simple and sometimes extreme solutions." In his view, the United States also should consider more thoroughly how its actions affects others.[4] A well-considered strategy for U.S. participation in major institutions should explain the basis for U.S. actions and prepare other members for likely future actions while reassuring them that U.S. decisions result from a broad-based, coherent analytical process. Other MDB shareholders may not agree with the conclusions of a U.S. strategy, but they should better understand the basis for them and be more able to anticipate likely future U.S. actions.

Initiate a Broader, More Substantive Dialogue with Congress

The executive and legislative branches need to have discussions on the MDBs that are broader in three aspects than current interactions. First, consultations should involve a wider group of congressional members from both parties to expand the range of perspectives represented and reduce the reliance on a few committee chairs to bring along their increasingly independent and skeptical colleagues. Broader consultations could also help to address the differences in congressional committee and subcommittee jurisdictions.

Second, the discussions should be more comprehensive. They should not be confined to the legislators' favorite topics and to budget issues, as is often the case now, but must look at the full range of issues needed to reach agreement on major U.S. priorities for the institutions. The executive branch should present its views on the future role of the institutions, offer its judgments on institutional performance, and identify future issues and tradeoffs among objectives so that legislators can ask questions and react to a comprehensive picture. Major decision points, including those on future U.S. funding, should be identified in advance, and the legislators should be given full opportunity to provide an informed response to the administration's proposed positions.

Finally, the consultations should regularly include group discussions among administration principals and members of Congress. If congressional consultations are confined to sequential talks with various legislators or staff, none will be fully aware of others' views or of the total context for decisions. Enough time should be allotted in the discussions for an exchange of views and debate, if necessary, in the hope of reaching as much agreement as possible on U.S. priorities.

Former congressman Matt McHugh has suggested that under the current organizational structure, these consultations could take the form of periodic informal discussions between the secretary of the Treasury and a bipartisan group of interested members of Congress. He thought the Treasury secretary's personal involvement would be important as would be the impression that the administration is committed to seriously considering the views of the congressional group.[5] Former Treasury deputy assistant secretary Susan Levine thought that consultations as thorough as possible should be held with Congress "before, during, and after" the executive branch concludes negotiations on new MDB funding replenishments.[6]

Comprehensive and substantive discussion among a group of concerned members of Congress should reduce the importance given to small "hobby horse" issues that occasionally have assumed undue prominence in the past. It would also offer the best hope of getting all the relevant political actors to agree at least on key elements of a U.S. position vis-à-vis the MDBs.

An arrangement quite similar to the one proposed here was advanced as part of the Carlucci Commission recommendations in 1983 for the foreign assistance program as a whole:

> Another major organizational recommendation concerns the establishment of a small, informal legislative-executive branch consultative group. . . . [We] recommend the formation of a group with a flexible membership, the composition of which would vary depending on the agenda to be discussed. We envisage a core group consisting of representatives of the Executive Branch and appropriate representatives of the committees of the House and Senate that are currently responsible for overseeing the program. . . .[7]

Establish a Means to Link U.S. Policies on MDBs More Closely to Policies on Related Issues

The United States should develop its policies toward MDBs within a broader policy framework regarding financial transfers to developing countries and economic policies toward these countries. This approach would end the current practice of formulating U.S. MDB policy largely without reference to U.S. policies toward other multilateral aid entities and the U.S. bilateral aid program. Although a number of alternatives would address this problem, the implications of many of them extend beyond this study to affect wider aspects of U.S. policy development. The relative desirability and workability of the various options will depend on a particular administration's broader structure and operating style, as well as the political landscape it faces.

Effective efforts to link MDB policy more closely to related policies should result in significant improvements in two areas. Policy formulation on the MDBs should

• include a broader range of U.S. interests as priority concerns of top policymakers—for example, whether MDB projects are delivering desired results on the ground and whether difficult institutional, governance, and social development issues are being addressed. In addition, the focus of the U.S. attention in improving the enabling environment for private sector development needs to be broadened beyond the current strong emphasis on macroeconomic and global financial issues to include more in-depth attention to microeconomic bottlenecks and to actual achievements in the areas of corporate governance, business practices, competition policy, and open trading regimes.

• establish a more effective means of resolving disputes over MDB policy in the executive branch. The current system does not function well to resolve disagreements among even the current narrow circle of players.

Three options for solving this problem will be explored, along with the advantages and disadvantages of each, as well as the circumstances under which each would work best. The options will be considered in order by the amount of change from the current executive branch organizational structure that would be involved.

Develop an Improved Coordination Structure among U.S. Agencies That Oversee Financial Transfers to Developing Countries. This option involves no major change in the responsibilities of the various agencies. The least disruptive solution to the fragmentation of policies and program priorities of the various U.S. financial transfer programs would be to develop a coordination structure strong enough to solve the problem. Each U.S. program would continue to be overseen by the same executive branch agency that currently manages it. The Treasury Department would continue to manage U.S. participation in the MDBs. The State Department's Bureau of International Organization Affairs would manage U.S. participation in UN aid agencies, and either USAID or the State Department would manage the bilateral aid program. The various other programs, such as aid for refugees and for reducing drug production, also would continue to be managed as they are now.

However, a stronger coordination mechanism would be established among the agencies overseeing specific programs. U.S. government agencies that do not oversee significant programs but have special perspectives and expertise, such as the Federal Reserve Board, the Environmental Protection Agency, the Office of the U.S. Trade Representative, and the Department of Agriculture, should also be involved.

This option has substantial history, vested interests, and systemic inertia working against it. A number of structures have been created to coordinate U.S. foreign assistance efforts, but have not been able to accomplish that objective. Likewise, most of the agencies overseeing aid programs are accustomed to and prefer running their own programs without the constraints that might be imposed by a strong coordination mechanism. One of the most compelling reasons to address existing fragmentation—the need to allocate resources more clearly on the basis of program performance—may appear threatening.

Although most of the agencies to be coordinated are likely to have doubts about a stronger coordination mechanism, the one apt to be most forceful in its opposition is the Treasury Department. As I.M. Destler writes in his recent study of the National Economic Council (NEC), "Treasury was universally regarded as more jealous of its prerogatives and less responsive to coordination than any of its cabinet counterparts. The NEC did not solve this problem—no White House staff has."[8]

Therefore, the success of the improved coordination option would require several bases of support that previous attempts have not enjoyed. The first prerequisite for success with this option is strong support from the most senior levels in the administration. The president and his top lieutenants must make it clear that they give high priority to the successful coordination of U.S. transfers to developing nations.

Second, a new coordination group composed of existing agencies would need strong initial oversight by an individual or group, with a clear mandate to perform this function. The president could name a trusted adviser as a "czar" for U.S. financial transfers to developing countries or charge a White House group such as the National Security Council (NSC) or the NEC with ensuring that the needed coordination occurs.

The presidential adviser or White House group should take the lead in examining the overall rationale and objectives for U.S. foreign transfers, establishing the role and relative priority of the various programs, looking at ways the programs could better reinforce each other, and instituting a system for monitoring performance and relating future budget allocations to performance. This individual or group should oversee the implementation of decisions, as well as ensure that coordination is continuing and disputes are being resolved appropriately.

This option is consistent with recommendations made on a number of occasions in the past. At the beginning of the Clinton administration, Representative Lee Hamilton, then chairman of the House International Relations Committee, suggested coordination of bilateral and multilateral aid policies by an NSC/NEC coordination mechanism in a memorandum to then deputy secretary of state Clifton Wharton.[9]

Under the Bush administration, the President's Commission on the Management of AID Programs had made nearly the same suggestion a few months before, proposing that there should be a subcouncil for foreign assistance of the proposed National Economic Council. It concluded: "To work, all [entities overseeing foreign assistance programs] must be brought to the table together. Therefore, the President must direct his new team to accept this arrangement and work within the new coordination structure. This will bring the multilateral banks and UN programs to the table with development, food aid, and technical assistance."[10]

The individual or group overseeing aid coordination would need to strike a fine balance—between playing an operating role on any of the programs, a role that most observers do not believe well suited to a White House coordination group,[11] and remaining involved enough to ensure that coordination takes place where needed. Many of the issues on which coordination is needed are somewhat technical matters, such as U.S. positions on MDB funding replenishments, U.S. approaches to institutional performance problems, and U.S. decisions on relative roles of various organizations. These issues, although critical to improved results of foreign transfers, are not the sort of high-visibility issues that usually occupy the time of senior White House and NSC/NEC officials. Nonetheless, they are likely to prove highly contentious among the various U.S. aid agencies.

The need to consistently address issues that have low political visibility and a longer time frame may be difficult for a White House–based group.[12] One alternative would be to rank any senior coordinating group on foreign transfers at the "deputies level" in the NSC/NEC structure, which means that participants would be under secretaries of cabinet agencies and heads of lesser agencies.

At the same time working groups of less senior officials could address important aid programming and performance issues that need improved coordination but do not require higher-level attention. One or two members of the joint NSC/NEC international economic staff could be given the responsibility to participate in and ensure the fair operation of the working groups.

Another issue requires assessing which agencies to include in the coordination group. Involving every agency that has some interest in a foreign transfer program would produce an unwieldy body. In one solution, a "core group" of agencies overseeing the major foreign transfer programs—Treasury, State, USAID—would be involved in all aspects of the coordination process (as well as, of course, the White House representative), while a broader group would consider more general issues or those involving particular concerns of the other agencies.

The option of developing an improved coordination structure among U.S. agencies that oversee financial transfers to developing countries has the following advantages:

- If the agencies involved have sufficient incentive to make the new mechanism work, this option could result in substantially improved coherence of U.S. foreign transfer programs.
- By involving a broader range of U.S. agencies in decision-making on foreign transfer programs, this option better recognizes the multiplicity of U.S. interests in the MDBs and other programs.
- By maintaining the Treasury Department's role as the agency in charge of management of U.S. participation in the MDBs, this option retains the link between MDB and IMF policy (as Treasury is also in charge of U.S. policy regarding the IMF) and with broader U.S. economic policy. However, it may also encourage continuation of the current tendency to regard the MDBs as "cash machines" for the IMF, rather than as agencies with different purposes.
- This option is the least disruptive because it makes few structural changes in how U.S. foreign transfer programs are managed.

This option also has the following disadvantages:

- Unless strong incentives are created to encourage support, this option probably would be opposed, and the role of the coordination mechanism minimized, by the agencies in charge of the various programs. Therefore, this option could prove ineffective.

• Arrangements that call for White House officials unconfirmed by Congress to coordinate powerful cabinet agencies face obstacles and depend for success on transitory relationships.

• A White House–based coordination mechanism would add an additional layer to MDB and other foreign assistance policymaking.

• Coordination among aid programs, even if improved, may not go far enough toward establishing well-integrated policy development for U.S. foreign transfers.[13] It also may not provide a strong mechanism for determining comparative performance and allocating funding to the most effective programs.

Consolidate Responsibilities for Foreign Transfers in the State Department (Including Lead Responsibility for the MDBs). The second option for solving the fragmentation problem is to consolidate oversight of long-term foreign transfer programs in the State Department.[14] This option, which would include changing lead responsibility for the MDBs, would build on congressional sentiment for concentrating more responsibility for various aid programs in the State Department.

Almost everyone who suggests this option indicates that it intrinsically involves a major change in State's current organization and focus. Therefore, the option might be best suited to a new administration that could select a new State Department leadership team with perspectives and skills appropriate for a changed State Department orientation.

Changes in global conditions have raised cross-cutting issues—in economics, business, crime, drugs, environment, and health—to much greater importance in U.S. international relations than in the past. A second deputy secretary of state position could be created to address such issues. In the context of increased State Department focus on these longer-term issues, it might make sense to place responsibility for all types of long-term foreign transfers in this part of the State Department. Under this scenario, responsibility for the MDBs, bilateral aid, UN aid programs, refugee aid, and antidrug programs would all be placed here. (Treasury's International Development Bank Office and all of USAID would be transferred, and within the State Department, the Economic and

Business Bureau, all of the Global Affairs complex, and the economic and functional parts of the International Organizations Bureau would report to the new deputy secretary.)

Key to achieving the objective of this change would be changes in leadership mindset and personnel policies to raise the State Department focus on long-term U.S. international objectives and interests to a level more in line with the department's current concentration on short-term political and country relationship priorities. Changes would be needed in State Department personnel policies that reward highly versatile and well-spoken generalists rather than those with in-depth expertise in a subject area or those skilled in the management of complex programs. Instead, the part of the State Department reporting to the new deputy secretary would depend for its success on attracting and retaining the highest quality expertise and analytical skills in key subject areas and on securing the services of top-flight managers for foreign transfer programs.

Some observers have expressed concern about whether a part of the State Department responsible for long-term, rather than country- or region-specific, issues could achieve influence in internal deliberations equal to the powerful and entrenched regional bureaus, and whether the established mindset of the talented cadre of career foreign service officers could be changed to give greater weight to considerations other than those of country relations and short-term political issues. Major concern was also expressed about the State Department's shortcomings in the area of program management and oversight. An administration adopting this option would need to select senior State Department appointees with the toughness and tenacity to reorient long-established priorities and elements of the department's organizational culture. As Jeffrey Garten of Yale University recently wrote, "The State Department's historic tendency to downplay the importance of economics in foreign policy runs deep in its culture, but that will have to change radically if America's broad foreign policy interests are to be served."[15]

Even if the major U.S. foreign transfer programs are brought together under the State Department, a coordination mechanism will still be needed to factor in the perspectives and expertise of other relevant U.S. agencies, such as the Treasury and the Federal Reserve on financial issues, the United States Trade Representative on trade issues, EPA on environmental issues, the Commerce Department on business issues, and the Department of Agriculture on agricultural matters.

The option of consolidating U.S. long-term foreign transfer programs, including the MDBs, under a reconfigured State Department has substantial advantages:

• By giving the policy formulation and decisionmaking role on most foreign transfer programs to one entity, this option should foster the formulation of a clearer U.S. rationale and strategy for such transfers. It should also encourage clearer U.S. choices about the roles of the various programs, more rigorous comparisons of performance, and budget choices based on relative track records.

• Because it consolidates the management of most aid programs, this option should provide for more rational allocation of U.S. personnel resources to better support the most important programs, such as the MDBs, and for better sharing of specialized expertise. It should permit budgetary savings by eliminating redundancies.

• This option should provide a clear decisionmaking process for differences of opinion on MDB and other aid issues, with the relevant deputy secretary of state, and, occasionally, the secretary, as the key decisionmakers. For disputes with other cabinet departments, a presidential decision would be needed.

• By placing the major U.S. transfer programs in an institution charged with doing cutting-edge analytical work on global problems, this option should ground U.S. policy toward all foreign transfer spigots in better knowledge of the global context and areas where available funding could have an important impact. The analytical reach of this part of the State Department should be comprehensive enough to provide significant background in most areas where the MDBs are active, from economic issues to environment, business, governance, and social sector development.

• This option would provide significant support for a reorientation of the State Department to better emphasize long-term, cross-cutting issues, a reorientation that many believe desirable in its own right.[16] It would strengthen the importance of functional expertise in the State Department's personnel system.[17]

This option has the following disadvantages:

• By placing the MDBs under the State Department, this option could lead to use of the institutions for short-term political objectives to an undesirable extent. Political issues have always affected U.S. policy toward the MDBs, but usually only in matters deemed critical to national security. Placing U.S. MDB policy under State could encourage the use of MDB policy for minor political objectives, which would erode the banks' economic and technical character. Some believe that clear policy delineation and the selection of appropriate leadership would minimize this danger.

- This option would require the State Department to develop improved management capabilities for the aid programs the United States manages directly and, in the case of the MDBs, improved capacity to oversee the operations of large and complex organizations. It would require changes in the State Department's personnel system to incorporate and promote officers with different skills, especially in-depth knowledge in a number of substantive areas.
- Because this option would remove the MDBs from the Treasury Department's direct oversight, it could lead to inconsistencies in U.S. policies on the MDBs, the IMF, and other international financial issues. On the other hand, it might lessen the temptation for Treasury policymakers to view the MDBs as ready sources of cash to supplement IMF and other short-term stabilization programs.
- This option, because it calls for significant changes in agency responsibilities and in the organizational structure of the State Department, would be more disruptive and take longer to implement than the first option.

Consolidate Responsibilities for Foreign Transfers, Including MDB Transfers, in a New Entity in Charge of International Economic Affairs. This option is based on the premise that international economic issues are rapidly achieving parity with, or even overtaking, political and military ones as determinants of U.S. security and welfare. For example, more than one-third of America's economic growth now comes from exports, and it is estimated that more than 16 million jobs are supported by overseas sales.[18] Therefore, international economic issues should not remain the purview of the current scattered group of cabinet departments and independent agencies that do not look at the whole picture or assess tradeoffs among U.S. economic interests and often fail to coordinate with each other. Also, these issues are now too important and too distinct to be left to departments whose primary concerns are international political and security issues (the State Department) or domestic finance and taxation (the Treasury Department).

Advocates of this option think that the fragmentation of U.S. policy on transfers to developing countries is a subset of a bigger problem—that is, the fragmentation of policy functions for many international economic issues.[19] Also, the National Economic Council, formed at the beginning of the Clinton administration to coordinate economic policy, remains thinly staffed and partially occupied with domestic issues. Something more is thus needed to formulate a coherent and carefully analyzed U.S. approach to the opportunities and challenges presented by the globalization of economies and financial markets.

This option calls for consolidating into a new cabinet department a much broader group of U.S. agencies active in international economic areas than just foreign assistance agencies, or than is called for in the prior option. Agencies to be aggregated into a new international economic affairs department would include the international part of the Treasury Department, the economic affairs bureau of the State Department, the parts of the State Department that oversee UN and refugee aid, the Office of the U.S. Trade Representative, part of the Commerce Department, USAID, and smaller agencies in the international economic area such as the Export-Import Bank, the Overseas Private Investment Corporation (OPIC), and the Trade and Development Agency (TDA).

Obviously the implications of this option extend well beyond this study, and considerations of its impact on MDB, or more general, foreign assistance policy are not likely to determine how it is viewed by decisionmakers. It would provide a solution, however, to the problem of fragmentation of the parts of the executive branch overseeing transfers to developing countries.

Advocates of this option believe that consolidating economic functions in the State Department could not achieve the objectives they seek. The top leadership at State is likely to be too distracted by international political and security issues, they argue, to do justice to economic issues.

In this option, the various types of U.S. foreign transfers would be placed under the policy umbrella of overall U.S. foreign economic policy and, specifically, U.S. economic policy toward the developing world. The United States could choose to support foreign transfer programs that filled priority gaps in moving toward

U.S. objectives and would attempt to steer multilateral institutions like the MDBs in directions consistent with those objectives.

All the major aid spigots would be part of the new department, so presumably coordination among them could be much closer. Expertise in a variety of areas, including such noneconomic concerns as social and environmental issues, could be shared more broadly than under the current fragmented structure. In the case of the MDBs and the other aid vehicles, however, a broader coordination process would still be needed to factor in the political interests of the State Department, the financial and economic perspectives of the Federal Reserve Board, as well as the concerns of other agencies such as EPA and the Department of Agriculture.

The United Kingdom recently changed its aid policymaking process somewhat in the direction of this option. It established a Department for International Development that is independent of the British Foreign Office and has a seat in the British cabinet. The head of the new department, who is also the UK's governor of the MDBs, has announced an objective of the new department to be the pulling together of a more coherent UK policy toward developing countries. However, the new UK department only addresses economic policy toward developing countries, rather than international economic policy more generally, as is proposed in this option.[20]

Consolidating responsibilities for foreign transfers, including MDB transfers, in a new entity in charge of international economic affairs has the following advantages:

- This option would elevate the importance of the international economic and financial issues increasingly important to the welfare of Americans and should encourage greater coherence in U.S. policy choices.
- By clearly giving the policymaking role on most foreign transfer programs to one agency, this option, like the prior option, would make more likely the formulation of a clearer rationale for U.S. foreign transfers and performance comparisons among U.S. aid spigots.
- Also, like the previous option, this option should realize budget savings on redundant functions as agencies combine and as the sharing and allocation of expertise among U.S. aid programs improve.

• This option would provide the most thorough grounding for MDB and all foreign assistance policy in new international economic developments, including new trends in trade, business, finance, and investment. The option has advantages over the second option because it includes in the consolidated agency all of Treasury's international functions, including oversight of the IMF; the trade policy function; and the private sector "transaction-oriented" agencies (the Export-Import Bank, OPIC, TDA). It would be especially suitable if initiatives to merge the World Bank and the IMF were adopted.

This option has the following disadvantages:

• Inconsistencies could occur between U.S. foreign economic policies and policies in the international political/security area if presidential decisionmaking on disputed issues were to falter.

• By separating international economic affairs from the rest of the Treasury Department, U.S. policy on international financial issues could become separated to an undesirable extent from policy on domestic economic and financial issues.

• Placing the MDBs and other aid agencies in a foreign economics department could result in an overemphasis on economic, business, and financial issues at the expense of other considerations (for example, social or environmental concerns). Appropriate leadership selections might mitigate this concern.

• Because this option would involve a major change in the functions of many executive branch entities, it would be disruptive and require large amounts of political capital to secure its approval.

Assessing the Options. The relative desirability of the various options to link U.S. MDB policy more closely to policies on related issues will depend on other organizational and personnel decisions made by an administration, as well as on the political climate at the time. The feasibility and desirability of the third option depend so heavily on how it affects matters beyond the scope of this study that it is not possible to make conclusions about it here.

The first option—improving coordination among agencies—is likely to succeed only if the administration can devote strong leadership, at least initially, to breaking through the expected entrenched resistance to effective coordination. Strong leadership would be especially important for the White House or NSC/NEC coordination group.

If such conditions do not exist, probably the only way to achieve the objective is to take more definitive action to change past bureaucratic patterns and mindsets. The most feasible way to do this would be to transfer the lead role on the MDBs to a significantly reconfigured State Department. Although this change poses risks, the administration has the power to minimize them with appropriate leadership selections. This option would be especially appropriate if an administration advocated deemphasizing the participation of the MDBs in short-term financial rescue operations.[21]

Make More Efficient Use of U.S. Government Resources for MDB Oversight

One of the clearest conclusions of this study is that the U.S. government is not monitoring the effectiveness of the MDBs closely enough to know if it is receiving maximum value for its investment. It is "penny wise and pound foolish" of the United States to allocate minimal personnel and other resources to watching over institutions into which it has poured more than $35 billion and to which it has contingent liabilities (in the form of callable capital) worth more than $65 billion.

The United States should substantially increase the effort it devotes to checking on MDB performance, to analyzing the more complicated issues facing the institutions, and to working with other members to adequately address problems. This does not mean that the United States must devote more total personnel resources to its foreign transfer programs; it does mean that it should allocate those resources more wisely, so that the more important programs, like the MDBs, receive the attention they require. It also means that better systems should be adopted for sharing expertise among the entities that manage foreign transfers in the U.S. government.

The following are specific changes that should be made in the use of U.S. resources to oversee MDB performance:

Give the Individuals Overseeing the MDBs a Mandate for More Proactive, Independent, and In-depth Scrutiny of MDB Programs. The United States needs to fully recognize that turning difficult tasks over to multilateral institutions and assuming that only light oversight is needed, especially during periods when the institutions are trying to fulfill more complex responsibilities, places burdens upon the institutions that they are often unequipped to handle. In the areas where the MDBs are having difficulty delineating their role or are experiencing persistent problems in identifying a feasible strategy, their shareholders, especially the largest shareholder, should independently analyze the causes of problems and articulate thoughtful views on solutions.

Specifically, the United States should pay more attention to a continuing flow of information that indicates the MDBs are having difficulty generating sustainable results from their large lending programs. In November 1997 the World Bank itself concluded:

> Some 60 percent of Bank operations still have only modest or less institutional development impact. The story on sustainability is somewhat less encouraging. The latest results indicate that the proportion of projects rated as having likely sustainability has inched upward from 46 percent in FY1990–95 to 48 percent in FY1996. . . . the overall result is sobering: in about half of Bank operations it is uncertain or unlikely whether the benefits will be sustained over the longer run.[22]

In the face of such information, the United States should increase its attention to the effectiveness of MDB programs. Instead of basing most of its limited monitoring and analysis on the planned use of MDB inputs, the United States should ascertain the results of MDB efforts and determine the cause of problems.

Besides monitoring results more than inputs, the United States should, following the lead of countries like Denmark and Norway, obtain independent information on the results of MDB operations rather than relying just on the MDBs' own reports (for example, the Danish Foreign Ministry's initiative to commission third party studies of MDB and other multilateral aid agencies' projects). The MDBs have been producing strikingly similar reports about their plans to solve problems with project effectiveness, in some cases for decades. It is very difficult to tell from reading these reports whether currently planned reforms differ from those planned in the past or whether they are likely to be more effective.

Also, the flow of information continues about major deviations of actual practice at some MDBs, especially in the field in developing countries, from the policies stated in official documents. In the World Bank, this problem has become such an issue that an effort has been made to designate some Bank policies as "safeguard policies" and stipulate that special efforts will be made to check on compliance with these. This initiative leads to obvious questions about the fate of the rest of the institution's official policies. According to the recent findings of one academic expert, "available evidence suggests that many projects continue to fall short of the Bank's own safeguard policies."[23] As an example of the problem, an internal World Bank memorandum, leaked to U.S. NGOs and the press in October 1998, reached the following conclusion about bank operations in Indonesia:

> A key problem relating to leakages in decentralized projects executed at the sub-national level is weak supervision of physical implementation in the field, by both central ministry technical staff and Bank missions. . . . The auditing requirements have been allowed to deteriorate into a superficial exercise; even an agency with overdue audits was not excluded from receiving new loans.[24]

Not only does the United States need to develop hard-hitting, independent analysis of MDB performance, it needs to use the analysis to formulate policy positions on MDB funding replenishments, budget allocations, and decisions on U.S. appointments to senior positions in the MDBs.

U.S. policymakers on the MDBs also need to broaden the type of analysis to which they accord priority attention on MDB issues. The inclination of current policymakers to give importance primarily to macroeconomic and financial considerations needs to be supplemented by greater concern about practical project implementation, institutional development, and social and environmental issues. Poor performance in any of these areas can negate the positive impact of MDB programs.

Insist That the MDBs Make Changes That Will Improve the Ability of Shareholders to Examine and Monitor Their Programs. It has long been recognized in the U.S. government that the MDBs utilize a number of procedural tactics to reduce shareholder scrutiny of their programs. The most common is the relatively short period between the release of upcoming project or policy proposals to shareholder governments and the vote by MDB executive boards on the proposal. The practice in some MDBs of "bunching" large numbers of their project votes during certain times of the year further ensures that the U.S. staff, when trying to review projects, cannot carefully consider even the more important or problematic issues.

The lack of adequate information and a less than user-friendly presentation of data by the MDBs are also problems. One of the reasons that the U.S. staff overseeing the MDBs focuses so much on inputs is a lack of readily usable material on either the status of projects being implemented or the results of prior projects. The United States and other MDB shareholders do not regularly receive reports on projects being implemented that are sufficiently substantive to allow status to be meaningfully assessed.[25]

MDB shareholder governments do receive large quantities of information from the departments in the MDBs whose function is to evaluate prior projects. However, the way this information is presented often makes it difficult for shareholders to reach conclusions on MDB results. Usually conclusions of evaluations on past projects are available only so long after the projects have been terminated that the institutions claim that any defects revealed are no longer relevant. Evaluation results usually are presented in opaque summary form. Often the methodology used is so complex that much time and sophisticated expertise is needed to decipher it, or results are couched in such unclear terms that most readers cannot derive a clear impression of the extent to which the institution is accomplishing key objectives.

Important elements of revitalized U.S. monitoring of the MDBs will be decisions on types of improved information on the status of ongoing projects and the results of past projects that are needed and a strategy to get the institutions to produce this information. For many years the U.S. staff working on MDBs and individual executive directors have pressed to receive MDB documents with longer lead times before executive board decisions, but the institutions resisted, and in most cases the United States did not give the issue high enough priority to obtain changes.

The final problem with the information the MDBs make available is their insistence that it be kept confidential within the shareholder governments. Most of the institutions do not routinely make available to the public detailed material on upcoming projects or on the results of specific past projects. If these documents were publicly available, a wide variety of groups, both in developed and developing countries, could provide their comments on the accuracy of the information and serve as a valuable "reality check" on the MDBs' own conclusions.

In the past, the U.S. monitoring system for MDBs has been stretched so thin that the lack of information was not a binding constraint. Indeed, often U.S. officers did not have time to digest the information that was available. However, if the oversight system is to be upgraded, these deficiencies in information availability will need to be tackled.

Make Available More Staff Resources with a Broader Array of Skills to Oversee MDB Operations. In addition to providing a more active mandate for staff charged with MDB oversight and receiving more usable data from the multilateral institutions themselves, the United States should devote more staff time to MDB oversight. Former Treasury deputy assistant secretary Lionel Johnson noted that there should be a team to manage the U.S. relationship with each bank rather than the single individual (in the Treasury Department) who now tries to cover all aspects of most institutions.[26]

The group working on the MDBs also needs to have more diverse skills beyond the current concentration in macroeconomics. Significant experience in developing countries is especially needed for a better understanding of what is feasible in the different environments in which the MDBs work. Also needed is expertise and in-depth experience in some of the most important areas of MDB operations—agriculture, small-scale enterprise, business regulation, energy, institutional development, and governance. Until the team overseeing the MDBs has greater practical knowledge of working conditions in developing countries and more substantive expertise in the areas in which they work, the United States will not be able to make the necessary judgments about the quality of their programs or useful suggestions about improving performance when problems surface.

Make Available Top Expertise When Problems Loom. When the United States is especially concerned about institutional performance or faces difficult decisions about future institutional roles, it should have mechanisms that enable it to draw on the most seasoned and knowledgeable expertise in the problem area. Such expertise could take the form of a senior U.S. government official with relevant experience, made available to serve on temporary assignment, or funding to hire a top-flight consulting firm to examine particular aspects of U.S. MDB policies. (Why, for example, have so many MDB financial sector reform loans failed, and what are the lessons for U.S. policy?)

There are a number of ways by which additional resources

for MDB oversight could be made available within the U.S. government. The most efficient way in some cases will depend on decisions taken on organizational placement of the MDB policy function. Regardless of the organizational option selected, the following steps should be taken:

- Make available modest additional resources to upgrade the communications technology used by the team working on MDB issues. This would include the technology to link all U.S. executive directors and the MDB oversight headquarters in regular videoconferences. It should also be possible to devise means to communicate more easily and rapidly with other MDB shareholders on key issues.
- Provide increased travel funding for the officers working on MDBs to regularly visit the institution they work on and a number of its projects. These project visits should include enough time to talk with both borrowing government officials and project beneficiaries to get a better picture of the environment in which MDB projects are carried out.
- Provide modest funding to hire top-quality experts for special studies and to participate with other member countries in joint studies of problematic aspects of MDB operations.
- Give U.S. embassies and USAID field offices in developing countries a mandate to play a more active part in U.S. MDB oversight. In most cases the U.S. Country Team is in the best position to obtain independent information on whether the major MDB programs in the country are progressing well or floundering. They should be tasked with putting additional effort into independently assessing progress on major projects.

For these steps to upgrade U.S. oversight of the MDBs, the funding should come from reallocating resources from lower priority aid programs or programs that are overstaffed in comparison to the funds at risk.

A decision to consolidate responsibilities for most U.S. foreign assistance, including the MDBs, either in the State Department or in a new international economic affairs department would make it easier both to reallocate U.S. staff to focus on the most important programs and to share specialized expertise. Sharing specialized expertise could be accomplished by putting the specialized staff from all aid programs—private sector specialists, agronomists, environmentalists, health specialists, financial experts, et cetera—into a functional unit whose services would be available across the range of U.S. aid programs. Also, it would be relatively easy to reallocate the most experienced and qualified officers either to the highest priority programs or to those facing the most difficult challenges.

However, if the first option of improved coordination among agencies is selected as a means of dealing with the aid fragmentation problem, reallocating and sharing expertise will be more difficult. In this case, one option would be the secondment of personnel from the more richly staffed aid programs, such as the bilateral aid program, to the more thinly staffed programs, such as the Treasury's MDB staff or the offices of U.S. executive directors at the MDBs. (This would have to be done on a much larger scale than has been tried in the past to have a significant impact.) Another option would be to create a combined foreign assistance technical office staffed with various types of technical experts who could be drawn upon by all the entities overseeing aid programs. This office could be administered by one agency or jointly managed by several. In both of these options, experts also could be drawn from other U.S. agencies with needed expertise, such as the departments of Agriculture and Energy, EPA, and OPIC.

If separate agencies are involved, however, the staff reallocation options are likely to prove contentious, and their success, like so many other aspects of this option, will depend on the ability of top administration officials to break through long-standing traditions of turf consciousness and rivalries among the agencies managing foreign transfer programs.

Establish a More Open Process

The U.S. government should develop mechanisms to consistently and systematically involve interested private groups in decision-making on MDBs. The more consistent involvement of a range of concerned private groups would give the U.S. official policy process the benefit of the additional knowledge and broader perspectives of these groups. Greater involvement of nongovernmental participants should enhance the mutually supportive elements of U.S. official policies and the actions of the private groups whose choices and decisions are assuming greater importance in U.S. interactions with developing countries. Broader nongovernmental involvement should also widen the base of support for eventual U.S. government policy choices regarding these institutions.

Moves in this direction would be consistent with the views of Congress, which recently mandated the establishment of a nongovernmental advisory committee on U.S. policy toward the IMF, and with the conclusions of two recent studies about the need to expand public participation in the formulation of U.S. foreign policy.[27]

Many different vehicles could be chosen to involve nongovernmental groups. The organizational effort required makes it logical for this broader involvement to be organized by the executive branch agency with responsibility for MDB policy. A serious effort should be made to involve a broad spectrum of groups that have an interest in the approach the United States takes to the MDBs and not just limit participation to the advocacy groups already well organized and skilled at lobbying on MDB issues. The interests that need to be involved include groups engaged in development work with their own funds, a variety of business and financial entities active in the developing world, labor unions, educational institutions, private foundations, and agricultural groups.

To establish a successful outreach mechanism will require excellent judgment. A mechanism will lack legitimacy if it includes only groups with the same perspective or is dominated by one point of view. If it includes too many peripheral groups that do not represent a constituency or take a serious interest, the mechanism is likely to bog down, and the interest of more important groups will be lost.

Important for maintaining the interest of key players in the nongovernmental groups will be the attitudes of executive branch and legislative policymakers. The outreach mechanism, while only advisory in nature, must be taken seriously by policymakers. If it is not, the participation of influential outside leaders and groups will decline, and the mechanism will fail to accomplish its objectives. A mechanism for public involvement that is handled badly or ignored by high-level policymakers could exacerbate the controversy about the U.S. role in the MDBs. On the other hand, a well-managed program for external involvement, in which private groups are involved in initial dialogue about U.S. goals and tradeoffs among objectives, could both substantially enrich the discussion and broaden support for the result.

Although there are many ways to structure such mechanisms for nongovernmental involvement in U.S. policymaking on MDBs, two possibilities would be an advisory committee to the executive branch agency responsible for U.S. policy and arrangements for public participation in formulating U.S. strategies for the MDBs.

Form a Nongovernmental Advisory Body for MDB Policy. A nongovernmental advisory body on MDB policy would systematically involve a broad range of nongovernmental interest groups in U.S. policymaking on the multilateral banks. It would also provide for regular dialogue to explore and sometimes debate the different interests and perspectives of these groups.

This advisory body should be large enough to include several representatives of the various types of nongovernmental interests—business, financial institutions, labor, private aid donors, advocacy NGOs, educational institutions, agricultural groups—but not so large as to hinder discussion and debate. Perhaps 25 to 30 members would be an appropriate size. Membership could rotate every several years to allow representatives of more institutions and companies an opportunity to participate. It would be helpful to have some representatives from various regions of the country to broaden perspectives and knowledge about the MDBs.

The group should meet three to four times a year to have time to discuss both broader issues on the MDBs' role and specific issues scheduled for decision in the governing bodies of the various institutions. Before the United States takes a position on a major issue in international negotiations, the group should discuss it fully.

A possible model for the advisory body could be the advisory committees on trade that have been maintained by the Office of the United States Trade Representative (USTR) since they were created by legislation in 1974. Several legal requirements for constituting advisory committees must be followed, but they are not burdensome. Although staff time is required to draft issues papers for the advisory group to review, USTR has not found the far more elaborate advisory committee structure (consisting of 33 different committees) that they manage jointly with several other agencies to be a large drain on staff resources. As is the case for the trade advisory committees, members of the MDB advisory body would serve without pay.[28]

The trade advisory committees are required by law to report to the president on all trade agreements, and the MDB advisory body could be required to report its views on proposed new MDB funding. As in the trade committees, members disagreeing with group conclusions could write a dissent to be published with the group's report.[29]

It would be desirable for this group to be selected by the administration in consultation with Congress and to include members representing different perspectives about the MDBs. The group should be bipartisan and optimally would reduce the sharp swings in policy that have at times characterized U.S. MDB policy after changes in electoral outcomes. Members of Congress and key staff should also be asked to participate. Based on the trade advisory committee experience, the key to success will lie in the selection of individuals with different points of view but who are willing to devote effort to the endeavor and are open-minded enough to work with those of different perspectives.[30]

Invite Public Participation in U.S. Strategy Formulation on Multilateral Institutions. Another way to broaden the involvement of interested public groups in U.S. decisionmaking on MDBs would be to announce U.S. government reviews of its strategy toward specific institutions and allow for a process of public comment. All groups, even those not well established in Washington or skilled at lobbying, could make their views known in a process that probably would better reflect the views of all the diverse civil society groups that might be interested than would the advisory committee structure. Similar issues generated useful comments from the public and a wide variety of nongovernmental groups when Australia used the process recently in developing its foreign aid strategy.[31]

Obviously, organizing a strategy formulation process that includes meaningful public involvement will be subject to pitfalls. Those managing the process must be both serious about involving the public and willing to consider with an open mind the views expressed. If they are not, the process could be easily manipulated so that only a fraction of those potentially interested, probably groups that largely agree with current policies or who benefit from those policies, would participate. Special care will need to be taken to provide enough unbiased background information and to frame issues in a way that does not predetermine the result or require such specialized knowledge that all but current insiders are discouraged from participating. If the process ends up with participation limited to those holding one point of view, it will quickly lose credibility and could exacerbate the frustration of groups that felt the process had been biased toward predetermined results.

One way to ensure that unbiased background material is available for strategy formulation would be to task agencies such as the Congressional Research Service, the General Accounting Office, or the Congressional Budget Office with providing it. Likewise, public policy institutes known for having different points of view could be asked well ahead of time to supply their analyses of key issues.

Public involvement in the formulation of U.S. strategies toward particular MDBs could result in useful two-way communication as a variety of potentially interested groups learn more about MDBs and the diversity of U.S. interests in them. At the same time, U.S. government policymakers could obtain valuable insights about the experiences of various U.S. groups with these organizations and about the priorities of U.S. citizens regarding the difficult tradeoffs often involved in transfers to developing countries. Including the perspectives of public groups in the formulation of U.S. approaches to individual multilaterals also puts pressure on the multilateral institutions to make better information available to the public.

Finally, the involvement of a variety of nongovernmental groups can safeguard the public interest and help ensure that a range of views is considered. The group dealing with the MDBs in the U.S. government, like all small groups of "insiders," can become too insular and fail to ask the hard questions or challenge long-held assumptions. In addition, the MDBs have increasingly become involved in activities that have the potential for substantially affecting the financial interests of many private groups. This reality increases the need to ensure that a broad spectrum of U.S. nongovernmental interests are represented and that the process of formulating U.S. policy is as transparent as possible.

Create a Better Selection Process for U.S. Appointees to Leadership Positions in the MDBs

One of the main ways the United States can influence the quality and direction of MDB operations is in the candidates it recommends for senior positions in the institutions. Identifying and selecting well-qualified candidates should thus be a major U.S. priority in the MDB policy process.

Long before the question of specific candidates arises, the United States should consider carefully the positions for which it wishes to have a voice in selecting candidates. Normally this should be part of the U.S. strategy process for a particular institution and should include considerations of the institution's role and recent track record. It also should be related to the confidence the United States has in the rest of the institution's management and in other important shareholders to select appropriate candidates. In some cases the United States may wish to trade the right to nominate a candidate for a position that either appears less important or is likely to be filled well by other members for the right to propose a candidate for a position that has been problematic or for which the United States has a uniquely well-qualified candidate. At times the United States may want to use leverage to support the appointment of well-qualified non-American candidates.

Besides a more strategic targeting of MDB positions for which to propose U.S. candidates, the United States needs to upgrade its process for selecting candidates. First, there needs to be a clearer recognition among policymakers of the nature of MDB leadership jobs. These positions often require rare combinations of substantive qualifications and personal characteristics. Most MDB leadership jobs require significant knowledge in specific areas, such as international economic development, finance, and regional issues, as well as experience in managing a large organization. Substantive knowledge in the areas of the institution's work is important not only for understanding the issues, but also for the perception it induces on the part of the institution's staff that the nominee is qualified for the position and will be capable of critically evaluating their recommendations and performance.

In addition, the nominee needs to thoroughly understand the role the United States plays in these institutions and the international political dynamics that affect the institution's governance. The individual needs to have the toughness to make difficult decisions, good judgment about priorities, and enough diplomatic skill to establish alliances and avoid squandering influence on frivolous matters. Because appointees to leadership positions in the MDBs usually face challenges to their authority, these individuals need the bureaucratic and political skills to manage such situations.

Leadership jobs in the MDBs are usually very visible within the institution and the international community, and, if the individual does not perform well, perceptions of U.S. leadership are affected. Also, because the positions are officially filled by actions of the MDB's executive board or are chosen by the institution's president, it is difficult and embarrassing for the United States to remove unsuitable selections once they have taken office.

In addition to recognizing the unique nature of these jobs, the United States needs a better process for seeking candidates and selecting among possible choices. A major cause of past U.S. problems with inappropriate selections has been the narrow circle of decisionmakers and the lack of checks and balances that normally comes with an organized decisionmaking process.

If the decisionmaking group on MDB policy is widened by the creation of an MDB policy advisory committee, more in-depth congressional consultations, and a broader decisionmaking circle within the executive branch, these changes should expand the group that can propose and debate the merits of candidates. To ensure that this broader group is appropriately involved, however, will require a more systematic and transparent process for selecting U.S. nominees. All the interests represented on the advisory committee and all the political perspectives seen in the congressional consultative group may not be pleased with each U.S. candidate. Yet the process of openly discussing the qualifications for the job and the advantages and disadvantages of possible choices should widen the pool of candidates considered and filter out those obviously unsuited for the position. The actual selection among the most qualified candidates should be made through the improved decisionmaking process established for all MDB issues.

Improve the Implementation of U.S. Policy

Many aspects of improving MDB policy implementation will flow from and depend on other elements of an improved policy process, especially clearer delineation of U.S. priorities and more timely decisionmaking. If these changes are made, the United States is much more likely to provide needed follow-up on the most important issues and have time to work to persuade other MDB members of the advantages of its positions. However, the following additional steps also would improve policy implementation.

Increase the Relative Emphasis Placed on Policy Implementation. Although many aspects of MDB policymaking need more time and attention, the need is relatively greatest for policy implementation. Many observers, including a number in MDB management positions, pointed to lack of timely and alert U.S. follow-up of its policy positions as a major problem for U.S. MDB policy. This problem tends to have a ripple effect. Every time the United States takes a position but makes little serious effort to be sure agreed actions have been taken, it tempts MDB staff, managers, and other members to regard all U.S. positions less seriously. Therefore, the U.S. tendency to come up with new priorities every year without checking on whether satisfactory actions have been taken on last year's priorities, or to passively accept a superficial MDB response, leads to the risk that no U.S. positions will be taken very seriously.

Not only does this ripple effect of unfulfilled MDB promises detract from good MDB performance, it contributes to the lack of public and congressional confidence in both the institutions themselves and in the executive branch's stewardship of them.

Ensure that U.S. Executive Directors Operate as Part of a Coordinated U.S. Government Team on the MDBs. U.S. executive directors in the MDBs play a number of important roles. If they have strong views on MDB policy and work skillfully to propound them, they often have a strong voice in setting policy toward their bank. Desirably, they represent U.S. views well to their fellow executive board members and the bank's management and staff. However, nowhere is the function of the executive director and his small staff more crucial than on policy implementation.

Good judgment about whether an institution is making satisfactory progress toward implementing new policies and improving its performance probably is more an art than a science, but proximity is a necessary element for practicing the art. Sound judgments on these issues require not only the greater access to MDB documents that executive directors and their staffs usually have, but more important, daily contact with the individuals in the MDBs whose actions will determine the success or failure of initiatives. This contact enables an executive director to put documents and policy statements in their proper context. An executive director who diligently pursues the implementation of agreed policies, who has good judgment about the role and performance of MDB officials, and who, with his staff, is well "plugged in" throughout the institution can have an unparalleled impact on successful policy implementation. On the other hand, the executive director who does not pursue key issues or fails to know whom to ask, or how to evaluate responses received, can have a major negative impact on policy implementation.

In view of the importance of their role, the U.S. executive directors should always be treated as key actors in the U.S. policy process. Their advice should be sought on major issues, and they should be thoroughly informed on all matters involving their bank. In turn, once decisions are made, it is the executive director's job to implement them actively, whether or not his views prevailed. Instances where U.S. executive directors failed to follow policy decisions by administration authorities have occurred in almost all administrations and should be treated very seriously because they undermine the decisionmaking process and create doubts about who speaks for the United States.

Recent improvements in communications technology make it easier to communicate with executive directors based in Manila, Abidjan, and London, and these should be fully utilized to develop a coordinated U.S. team dealing with the MDBs.

Develop More Systematic and Effective Frameworks for Consultation with Other MDB Members. Instead of leaving it more or less up to each new executive director or MDB policymaker to select or devise channels to relate to key counterparts on MDB policy, the United States should build and consistently maintain stronger frameworks for collaboration with other members.

The better policymakers understand the context for each other's views, including the domestic pressures each faces, and amass a body of shared understanding before key decisions must be made, the more likely difficult issues can be worked out. The United States should ensure that such good collaborative relationships become a central element of the MDB policy process rather than viewing such consultations as something to be done as time permits.

A more intense and systematic framework of consultation between the United States and other MDB shareholders in their capitals, which is likely to be facilitated by improved communications technology, would help keep attention focused on major U.S. priorities. It would reduce the instances in which U.S. policies are thwarted, not by strong opposition of other governments, but by lack of attention to an issue or the distraction of parochial concerns at an institution's headquarters.[32]

Conclusions

In the last two decades the MDBs have grown substantially in size, and their relative place in U.S. foreign economic policy has expanded even more. These institutions are now at the center of official U.S. relations with much of the developing world. At the same time, the institutions are being called upon to perform more difficult tasks and to meet higher performance standards. Close observers of the institutions from all positions on the ideological spectrum have expressed doubts about their response to this more challenging environment.

Meanwhile, the U.S. government's process of managing its participation in these institutions has changed hardly at all. In fact, the key characteristics of the process in the executive branch seem to have become more pronounced in the last several years.

The decisionmaking loop remains tightly circumscribed, usually a small group of senior Treasury officials. The extent of influential input from other parts of the executive branch, Congress, or public groups is limited.[33] This means that the perspectives and issues considered are restricted to the preoccupations of this group.

During the recent global economic crisis, a number of observers questioned whether this group had sufficiently deep understanding, especially of the political and institutional facets of the problems in the countries hit by the crisis. They contend that the problems that engulfed Indonesia, Korea, Thailand, China, Japan, Russia, and Malaysia stem from structural features that have deep roots in the countries' political, social, ethnic, and historical backgrounds. Meanwhile, the U.S. decisionmaking process did not ensure that perspectives were included from those who may have had better knowledge of these aspects of the problem.

Former defense secretary and World Bank president Robert McNamara, quoted in the *Wall Street Journal,* drew a parallel to U.S. decisionmaking on the Vietnam War three decades ago: "The parallel is that you have to dig deeply and understand your problems and do it early. We didn't understand the political or economic problems in Japan, Indonesia, or Russia early enough."[34]

A cover story in *Institutional Investor* made the same point: "This band of mostly like-minded men are pushing ever deeper into what for them are unknown areas—and putting the credibility of the two Bretton Woods institutions. . . increasingly on the line. . . . they are arguably out of their depth in matters of local politics and culture."[35]

In his recent article, "Lessons for the Next Financial Crisis," former Commerce Department under secretary Jeffrey Garten noted: "The worlds of finance and foreign policy need to be bridged. In the end, many of the biggest problems with financial management are political. . . . Better financial diplomacy could ease economic and political turmoil."[36]

The key decisionmakers on the MDBs also tend not to focus on these institutions very often. Preoccupied with other issues, the top decisionmakers tend to delegate even most issues concerning the MDBs' role, their performance in accomplishing basic objectives, and issues of accountability and transparency to the deputy assistant secretary and his overstretched staff. These issues are thus negotiated very differently with other shareholders and senior managers in the institutions.

Although the most senior Treasury officials are usually quite assertive in negotiating their top priorities in the MDBs (for example, terms, conditions, and timing of recent rescue packages), the less senior officials often have far less success in their negotiations on the operational and performance issues. For example, even as the executive branch was expressing a desire for greater MDB transparency and accountability, it has secured few major changes in these areas in the MDBs in recent years. The United States recently was forced to accept a weakening of the World Bank Inspection Panel, the creation of which was the centerpiece of the House Banking Subcommittee's 1993 initiative on MDB accountability.[37]

A former U.S. executive director at the World Bank recently summed up the result of the limited attention paid to MDB issues by top decisionmakers: "The chief reason these institutions remain essentially frozen in their late 1940s framework is that U.S. Treasury Secretaries. . . have never put serious reform at the top of their 'to do' lists."[38]

Another key characteristic of the MDB policy process is its ad hoc nature. Issues tend to be considered on an "as needed" basis, at times in such an informal way that proposed positions may not be examined in depth or subjected to the challenge and debate common in a more structured decisionmaking process.

Some believe that U.S. initiatives to get the MDBs to make available large sums to relatively wealthy borrowers as part of IMF stabilization packages may have been one of the matters that did not receive enough consideration. Did the United States thoroughly examine whether the contribution the MDBs could make—either financially, in view of the magnitude of private flows at issue, or intellectually, in view of the IMF's apparent dominance of the policy agenda—warranted the risk to the MDBs' capital and the costs to the institutions and their borrowers in terms of other programs? It can be argued that the dynamic between the wealthier developing countries, such as Brazil and Korea, and their private financiers is a complex one that is likely to be influenced by many diverse forces and events. Whether the MDBs' capital should be risked in short-term bailout packages that attempt to affect that dynamic seems to warrant more searching analysis and serious debate than it appears to have received in the U.S. government.[39]

Congressman Jim Leach, chairman of the House Banking Committee, noted on May 20, 1999:

> Efforts to improve crisis management and crisis prevention have resulted in a patchwork quilt of new lending and guarantee arrangements spreading throughout the IMF and the other IFIs. There are contingent credit lines, new emergency lending facilities at the IMF and regional development banks, "credit enhancements" for sovereign bond issues by borrowing countries, and other novel arrangements. . . . These new instruments. . . . make it less likely that the IFIs will finally undertake a much-needed focus on core competencies and value-added to the international system.[40]

U.S. policy on MDBs continues to be linked only tenuously to policy on other transfers to developing countries. The fragmentation of U.S. foreign assistance into multiple programs, only loosely coordinated with one another, supplies ammunition to the skeptics about all of the programs. The current organizational structure hinders the forceful articulation of a strong rationale that can stand up to challenge by critics, squanders possibilities for greater synergism among aid activities, and leads to confusion about the roles and the results of the various programs. It fails to foster the impression that the executive branch has a firm grip on why it is providing funds to developing countries and what those transfers are accomplishing.

The MDBs now stand at the heart of the U.S. relationship with many poor countries, and how the United States handles its role in these institutions is critical for their future. The United States needs a process for developing its policies toward them that is consistent with this responsibility.

5

Managing Multilateralism: Broader Implications of the MDB Experience

Obviously multilateral institutions differ, as does their political context. The U.S. policy formulation and implementation process must take account of these differences. However, it does appear that many of the lessons of experience in developing U.S. policy on the MDBs are relevant to the broader group of multilateral economic institutions such as the United Nations economic and social agencies, the IMF, and the World Trade Organization (WTO). The following are lessons of the MDB experience that appear to be more broadly relevant to U.S. participation in other multilateral institutions:

The United States Should Not Expect More from Multilateral Institutions Than They Can Deliver

A key to successful policies toward multilateral institutions involves realistically assessing both the general characteristics of multilateral institutions and the specific characteristics of each. The United States should therefore limit the issues it expects multilateral institutions to resolve to those within their capabilities—and those capabilities should be carefully analyzed. Issues that present intractable political, conceptual, or managerial problems probably cannot be addressed successfully by an international organization unless its largest members also are prepared to use their own political and material resources extensively, whether the issue at hand is negotiating peace in Bosnia or determining the role of foreign aid in the twenty-first century.

In addition, multilateral institutions should not be expected to select and define their own missions. In defining roles, the bureaucratic interests of the institution and its leaders are likely to differ substantially from those of its members, especially those members that are expected to provide the resources. If the large financial supporters of multilateral institutions do not exercise careful vigilance, many multilateral institutions are likely to try to expand their mandate and their bureaucratic reach onto ill-defined tasks, lower priority projects, or areas more properly the responsibility of other entities.

Finally, the performance of multilateral institutions should be actively monitored. Because multilateral institutions are further removed from the citizens whose taxes support them, it is especially important that member governments do not neglect their obligation to provide vigilant oversight on what the multilateral institutions are doing and how well they are doing it.

Often, however, the United States has failed to provide such oversight. In the case of a number of the UN foreign assistance agencies, as well as some of the UN technical agencies, the fragmented nature of U.S. foreign assistance means that U.S. oversight on these agencies is not informed by U.S. personnel knowledgeable about aid issues or about the technical matters the institutions address. Instead, for most of the UN agencies—including the United Nations Development Program (UNDP), the United Nations Children's Fund (UNICEF), the UN Fund for Population Activities (UNFPA), the UN Secretariat's Department for Humanitarian Assistance (DHA), the Food and Agricultural Organization (FAO), and the World Health Organization—the State Department's Bureau of International Organization Affairs takes the lead on many issues, especially those regarding their budgets and their roles in the UN system. In the case of FAO and WHO, the U.S. Department of Agriculture (USDA) and the Department of Health and Human Services (HHS) are supposed to play a technical oversight role.

In this situation, State Department officers, who are usually generalists rotating into this part of the State Department for tours of two or three years, usually do not have the expertise to know what the institutions should be doing or to judge the quality of their product. These officers, no matter how diligent, are at a strong disadvantage when trying to deal with UN agencies that have complex operating procedures and often do not provide transparent budget and performance data. Attempts by senior State Department officials to persuade AID to make available expertise in needed areas often have been rebuffed on the grounds of perceived lack of priority for AID's own programs.

In cases where U.S. domestic agencies with relevant expertise are supposed to help with oversight (USDA on FAO and HHS or WHO), some additional technical competence is brought to bear. Because the State Department has responsibility for UN agency budget oversight, however, questions sometimes arise about whether the U.S. technical agencies accord their role high enough priority and are sufficiently rigorous in their judgments about the UN agencies' performance.[1]

The former director of AID's humanitarian affairs bureau, who had extensive experience with a number of UN agencies, thinks part of the management problem with some UN agencies rests with the experience and focus of the people trying to oversee them:

> The members, even among Western democracies that should know better, do not hold the UN system to standards of managerial discipline and economic efficiency that they demand of their own bureaucracies. In part this is because a number of countries send diplomats who are unskilled in and uncomfortable with managerial, budgeting, accounting, and personnel systems to represent them in UN councils.[2]

To participate effectively in multilateral institutions, the United States needs to monitor the institutions' performance carefully, and to do so, must have an organizational arrangement in the U.S. government under which people sufficiently knowledgeable about the institutions' missions and their expected products are responsible for and motivated to provide such oversight.

The United States Should Review Its Participation in Each Institution Periodically and Develop a Clear Strategy

A periodic U.S. review of participation in each multilateral institution, starting from the perspective of requiring that continued participation be justified, should help to reassure the public that the United States is not contributing to entities that have lost their reason for existence. It will help also to keep the United States focused on what should be the most important functions of the various organizations in light of current conditions.

This review should concentrate heavily on institutional performance. Where reliable information on performance is not available, the review should consider the implications for U.S. participation.

When examining institutions whose relevance or performance is questionable, the review should realistically assess the chances for improvements, perhaps establishing time-phased benchmarks. In the case of institutions where continued substantial participation is warranted, the United States should develop a strategy to guide its participation over the next several years that determines the relative priority of various U.S. objectives.

This review and strategy process should include congressional participation and be open to interested public groups. This process would give the critics of particular multilateral institutions a vehicle through which to articulate their concerns. These concerns could be answered either by the institution itself or by its supporters. For controversial multilaterals, an open debate in which all can participate is probably better than having supporters talk only to sympathetic principals, who may not be fully aware of problems with the institution, while opponents raise their concerns with members of Congress or others, who may not be aware of all sides of the issue either.

In these reviews, the United States will need to make some difficult choices. To restore credibility to the multilateral institutions that are important to the United States and that are doing good work, the U.S. government may need to demonstrate to skeptics that it is prepared to take tough decisions when either erosion of institutional roles or continued poor performance makes this appropriate.

The United States Should Work to More Clearly Define the Relative Roles of Multilateral Institutions

One of the problems in garnering greater U.S. support for multilateral institutions seems to be the large number of institutions working in the same areas and the lack of clarity about their roles with respect to each other. In the case of the MDBs, their role compared with the IMF's has become increasingly blurred as the MDBs approve funding for short-term financial stabilization. Also, as problems with developing country institutions have become increasingly serious roadblocks to development, several of the MDBs have moved heavily into technical assistance, traditionally the specialty of the UNDP. In the case of UN agencies, major questions have long been raised about the relative roles of different entities, and the fights over jurisdictions among some agencies are legendary. Recently the relative roles of the UN's Conference on Trade and Development (UNCTAD) and the World Trade Organization (not a UN agency) have been questioned.

The United States obviously cannot resolve by itself such questions of relative roles and jurisdictional boundaries among multilaterals. It would be helpful, however, if the United States could have a clearer vision of how it sees their relative roles. As discussed earlier, one of the problems that hampers the development of such a vision is the fragmentation of jurisdiction over international economic issues, and especially foreign aid matters, within the U.S. government. Yet this problem is not the only one, because the World Bank and the IMF, both overseen in the U.S. government by the Treasury Department, provide one of the most persistent examples of the confusion of institutional roles. Various U.S. executive directors and their respective backstop offices in Treasury have argued about the appropriate roles for the World Bank and the IMF for years without a clear resolution.

Many observers believe that one of the UN's critical problems is the lack of a clear, consistent view of its role on the part of its most important members. A new study of the relationship between the United States and the UN concluded that "no (UN member) state was less consistent than the United States."[3]

In the case of the UN agencies, not only are relative roles not clear, but coordination among the similar UN agencies has long been a problem. One former senior U.S. official with long experience working on UN issues said that, although the United States has long and publicly espoused improved coordination among UN agencies, the United States "never got to the point where it put teeth into its injunctions for better coordination," and, as a result, "it didn't happen."[4]

If the United States were to succeed in developing a clearer vision of its own about relative institutional roles, perhaps through the strategy formulation process, it could then try to create a coalition of other key members in support of more clearly defined roles. This would help multilateral institution managers to plan their programs more effectively and should permit more persuasive explanations to Congress and the public about why the various institutions are needed.

The United States Needs a Clear Decisionmaking Process on Issues Affecting Multilateral Institutions

The problem that has hindered U.S. policy formulation on the MDBs—the lack of a clear U.S. decisionmaking process—also has been a problem in the case of other multilateral institutions. The United States appears to have an especially difficult time making up its mind in a timely fashion about whom to support in battles over multilateral institution leadership posts. On a number of occasions, the United States has dallied so long in making up its mind about which candidate to support in leadership contests in multilateral institutions that it lost influence both in the decision and, subsequently, with the winning candidate (for example, the election several years ago of a director-general in the FAO).

Some observers believe that many of the problems of coordination among UN agencies are exacerbated by unresolved internal disagreements in member countries between the various government entities that play leading roles in determining policies toward different parts of the UN system. The Danish government's *Plan of Action for Active Multilateralism* concludes:

> There would be no problem [concerning inadequate coordination among UN agencies] if individual member countries took consistent positions in the different [UN agency] governing bodies, but this is not the case, because, for one thing, in many countries there is no effective coordination between the ministries of foreign affairs and the specific ministries that typically head the delegations at meetings in the [UN] specialized agencies.[5]

In the U.S. government, this was evident in the case of the FAO, where in the face of problematic FAO leadership, the departments of State and Agriculture took different approaches for a number of years. The lack of a clear decisionmaking process also may have been a factor behind the inconsistency in U.S. policy toward UN management weaknesses over the past several decades as the institution's current management problems were accumulating.[6]

The United States Should Establish a Deeper Dialogue between the Executive and Legislative Branches on Multilateral Institutions

One of the most important things the United States needs to do to improve its participation in multilateral institutions is to establish a more productive dialogue between the executive and legislative branches. This dialogue should be structured to continue regardless of which party controls the two branches of government.

A number of changes could assist in such an effort. Before the executive branch makes funding commitments, much more broad, interactive, and substantive consultations should take place with Congress. However, if the executive treats the results of such consultations seriously when it negotiates U.S. funding commitments, legislators should feel greater responsibility to try to honor them. To do otherwise weakens the voice of the United States in the institution and causes difficulties for U.S. allies and managers in the institutions. However, this change will not occur unless the executive makes a serious effort to consult with and be responsive to interested members of Congress, including those with whom it does not agree.

Also, political actors from all sides should restrict their efforts to turn a number of essentially uncontroversial issues concerning multilaterals into political issues. The practice of holding multilateral institution funding hostage to actions on unrelated issues is one example. However, this practice is likely to diminish if an improved policymaking process results in U.S. financial support only for multilateral institutions that are widely perceived to be playing an important role and doing a good job. To hold funding for well-regarded programs hostage is less appealing than for those about which large segments of the public have major doubts anyway. Likewise, political actors should stop trying to portray legitimate questions about the effectiveness and future role of some multilateral institutions as isolationism or a lack of concern for the welfare of foreign citizens.

Although establishing a more effective executive-legislative consultative framework on multilateral institutions is likely to be time-consuming and difficult, nothing is more important for improving the U.S. policy process. As the former president of the United Nations Association of the United States recently wrote:

> It would be enormously helpful if the U.S. government could learn to speak with one voice about these issues. . . . Our message gets garbled by the frequent struggles between executive and legislative branches of the U.S. government and by endless partisan bickering. . . . UN reform need not be a partisan issue. Independents, Republicans, and Democrats should be able to rally around a common reform agenda that could appeal to like-minded member states.[7]

The United States Should Use Its Influence More Effectively

The files of the U.S. General Accounting Office's international affairs division are filled with reports dating back at least two, and sometimes three, decades that detail management problems with various UN agencies, especially a lack of accountability and the lack of knowledge of program results. At the end of each report is a section in which the executive branch administration of the day reports on its plans to remedy the problems, in unfailingly upbeat and persuasive prose. After reading a selection of these reports, the reader is left with many questions about what could have happened to all of these plausible and commendable initiatives. The reader is faced with two options—either to conclude that at least some multilateral institutions are not readily amenable to "fixing," even by their largest and most influential member, or that something went very wrong in the U.S. government's efforts to implement its reform agenda.

Although the answer cannot be known with certainty, it is possible to note some of the problems that have weakened U.S. efforts to use its considerable influence to spur multilateral institutions to perform their functions better. Former World Bank chief economist Anne Krueger discussed the general problem: "U.S. influence in the multilateral institutions has been less constructive and weaker than might have been hoped. . . . Most U.S. policies toward multilaterals have been incoherent and reactive, born of neglect and suspicion."[8]

The first problem with the use of U.S. influence in multilaterals has been, as Krueger noted, that it often has not been based on a coherent strategy with the strongest U.S. leverage devoted to the most important issues. Instead, the United States often has wasted political capital on less important issues or issues of only transitory importance. Sometimes the ineffective use of U.S. leverage has resulted from the poor relations of successive administrations with Congress on multilateral issues, which may have led the executive branch to seek additional congressional support by devoting much capital to issues important to one or two members, or their staffs, at the expense of other matters. The United States has used heavy leverage to try to hold multilateral institution leadership positions for Americans who were not able to deliver commensurate returns in improved institutional performance.

Several years ago a senior State Department official noted that the United States seldom raised the issue of management problems in the UN system with a previous secretary general in spite of growing U.S. concerns in this area. Because the United States always had such a long list of current political issues to raise, the management issues were never discussed. A UN official who was then present in a number of the senior-level meetings confirms this account.[9]

Even in cases where the United States has raised at times the more important continuing issues, it has often failed to focus on them consistently enough to achieve changes. Multilateral institutions are complex, and even their most motivated and skilled leaders need time to make significant improvements. If important members like the United States fail to follow through in pushing for and monitoring changes, the people in the institution who are trying to make the changes are likely to get discouraged or fall victim to forces opposed to reforms. It is especially counterproductive for the United States to give the impression that it has a rapidly changing list of priorities in multilateral institutions, because it gives those opposed to U.S. reforms the idea that they need only stall and the United States will move on to something else.

The United States Should Better Use Its Influence over Appointments to Senior Positions

As discussed earlier, few decisions are more critical for the functioning of a multilateral institution than the choice of its senior leadership. For historical and other reasons the United States always has played an enormous role in selecting the leadership of many multilateral institutions, in addition to that of the MDBs.

Ironically, in the UN system, the target of much criticism in the United States for poor management and inconsistent performance, the United States always has been responsible for the selection of a large number of the most senior leaders. Until recently, in the foreign assistance area, Americans nominated by the U.S. government headed three of the five major UN funds and programs. The United States has consistently filled the position of UN under secretary general for management.[10] Not only has the United States nominated candidates for a large number of UN leadership posts, it has been willing to exert heavy pressure to secure the posts for its nominees even to the point of annoying a number of allies.[11]

In view of persistent problems with a lack of information on program results, murky accounting practices, and untransparent procedures in the UN system and the strong U.S. criticism of these, the U.S. policy toward UN leadership appointments merits reexamination. Some believe that part of the reason the United States has not taken a tougher line in the past on UN management problems has been an obviously shortsighted desire to avoid embarrassing U.S. appointees, and in some cases U.S. appointees simply turned away U.S. approaches urging reform of their agencies.[12]

As part of the process of developing U.S. strategies toward the most important multilateral institutions, the United States needs to consider carefully which leadership positions it sees as priorities for U.S. nominees. In doing so the United States should consider whether it has a candidate that can make a real improvement in the agency's programs and management practices and the likelihood that other members would produce equally well-qualified candidates. In the current climate of congressional and public skepticism about multilateral institutions, the last thing the United States needs is to expend significant political capital to influence leadership decisions in troubled multilateral agencies for candidates who do not possess the extraordinary qualities needed to turn a problematic institution around.

The United States Should Open Its Policy Formulation Process to Greater Participation by Nongovernmental Actors

The role of government is rapidly shrinking as a share of all interactions between Americans and other nations, and the role of private groups is rapidly expanding. One of the problems facing U.S. policymaking on multilateral institutions is the perceived unpopularity of the institutions with the public. Evidence suggests that, at least in the case of foreign aid, the American public is not hostile to the concept of assisting foreigners, but rather has little confidence that some of the major public sector aid institutions are undertaking effective programs. In this situation, it makes sense to include private groups in the U.S. policy formulation process to a far greater extent than in the past.

As noted in the case of the MDBs, there are a number of possible alternatives for factoring in the opinions and concerns of private groups in a meaningful way, but many will depend on the nature of the multilateral institution and the types of private groups interested in it.

The perspective of private groups could be especially helpful in the case of some of the smaller multilateral agencies whose claims that their products are valued by U.S. consumers are often debated within the U.S. government. Opening up the U.S. policy formulation process would enable comments to be solicited from groups that may benefit and would also allow critics to air their doubts. This process should result in better-informed U.S. decisions and in more public confidence that U.S. decisions are not being made behind closed doors.

An effort to include public input in U.S. decisions should be accompanied by much stronger U.S. efforts to get multilateral institutions to be more transparent, whether their lack of transparency takes the form of secretiveness, as is the case with the MDBs and the IMF, or the form of excessive complexity of financial records or operating procedures, as seems to be the situation with some other multilateral institutions.

President Clinton's remarks before the World Trade Organization in Geneva in May 1998 were an excellent step toward securing greater transparency in this organization: "We must modernize the WTO by opening its doors to the scrutiny and the participation of the public."[13] Recent congressional initiatives also may improve the transparency of the IMF. They should be followed by more serious U.S. initiatives to improve the transparency of other multilateral institutions.

In pushing for substantially greater transparency in multilateral institutions, the United States may need to use considerable political leverage. Institutional inertia and the perceived interests of some other members will be forces against change. On the other hand, if the United States carefully and sensitively launches such a campaign and lets other members know that this initiative has top-level support, it is hard to imagine that real progress cannot be made in most institutions. A multilateral institution that is prepared to risk the support of its largest member so it can maintain incomprehensible accounting systems and secret deliberations will probably not attract other democratic member nations as well, especially if such resistance becomes a high profile, public issue.

AS THE NEW CENTURY BEGINS, debate will probably continue about multilateral institutions and the U.S. role in some of them. This debate will be fairer and more accurate if there is stronger focus on how the nature and quality of U.S. participation in these institutions affect the performance of the institutions and the results Americans derive from them.

The ability of Americans, from government policymakers to public groups across the country, to accurately assess the advantages and disadvantages to multilateral approaches is likely to increase in significance. As the United States considers its future foreign policy in an increasingly interconnected world, its ability to make sound decisions about multilateral institutions and, when warranted, to exert effective leadership in them will become ever more important.

Harvard Professor Devesh Kapur recently wrote: "Ultimately, the limitations of multilateral institutions. . . reflect the limitations of those nation-states that created them. And, if. . . power should go hand-in-hand with responsibility, then those states with the most power in these institutions must bear the blame for their failings and assume the greatest responsibility for their rejuvenation."[14]

Notes

Notes to Introduction

1. "Fifty years is enough" was adopted in 1994 as the slogan of a coalition of nongovernmental organizations advocating major change in the World Bank at the time of its fiftieth anniversary.

2. Danish Ministry of Foreign Affairs, *Plan of Action for Active Multilateralism*, Copenhagen, 1996, p. 36.

3. World Bank, *The Strategic Compact: Renewing the Bank's Effectiveness to Fight Poverty* (Washington, D.C.: World Bank, February 13, 1997), ii.

4. Jimmy Burns and Frances Williams, "Refugees' Agency Lost in Wilderness of Bungling and Waste," *Financial Times*, July 29, 1998, p. 9.

5. George P. Shultz, William E. Simon, and Walter B. Wriston, "Who Needs the IMF?" *Wall Street Journal*, February 3, 1998.

6. Recent examples include blame heaped upon the UN by the great powers in Somalia, Bosnia, and Rwanda as discussed in Robert Oakley, "Using the United Nations to Advance U.S. Interests," and John Hillen, "Getting the UN Military Operations Back to Basics," in *Delusions of Grandeur: The United Nations and Global Intervention*, ed. Ted Galen Carpenter (Washington, D.C.: Cato Institute, 1997), 88, 121. Another example concerns assessing blame for UN management problems, which is discussed in Andrew Natsios, *U.S. Foreign Policy and the Four Horsemen of the Apocalypse* (Westport, Conn.: Praeger/CSIS, 1997), 78.

7. George P. Shultz, "Ideas, Institutions, Policies" (Ely Lecture: American Economic Association, Washington, D.C., January 6, 1995), 12.

8. This issue is specifically raised concerning Japan in Dennis T. Yasutomo, *The New Multilateralism in Japan's Foreign Policy* (New York: St. Martin's Press, 1995), 101.

Notes to Chapter 1

1. Organization for Economic Cooperation and Development (OECD), Development Assistance Committee, *Development Cooperation,* 1999 edition (Paris: OECD, 1999), A42.

2. Congressional Research Service calculations based on AID data, June 14, 1999.

3. Greg Ip, "Capital Markets Help Shorten Crises," *Wall Street Journal,* April 5, 1999; Khozem Merchant and Geoff Dyer, "Brazil Set to Return to Capital Markets," *Financial Times,* April 16, 1999, p. 1; Michael M. Philips, "Apocalypse? No," *Wall Street Journal,* April 14, 1999, p. 1; Ian Katz and Geri Smith, "The Latins Are Back in the Game," *Business Week,* April 26, 1999, p. 54; George Graham, "Bank Loans Cut to Emerging Economies," *Financial Times,* May 3, 1999, p. 4.

4. Devesh Kapur, John P. Lewis, and Richard Webb, *The World Bank: Its First Half Century; Volume I: History* (Washington, D.C.: Brookings Institution, 1997), 48–49.

5. Because of limitations on the public availability of data from the MDBs, there are no broad independent studies of the results of their programs. Probably the most complete and credible information is contained in the following series of "portfolio reviews" done by the institutions themselves from 1992 to 1994: *Report of the Portfolio Management Task Force in the World Bank* (Wapenhans Report) (Washington, D.C.: World Bank, 1992); *Report to the Task Force on Improving Project Quality in the Asian Development Bank* (Schultz Report) (Manila: Asian Development Bank, 1994); *Managing Effective Development in the Inter-American Development Bank* (Tapoma Report) (Washington, D.C.: Inter-American Development Bank, 1993); and *The Quest for Quality in the African Development Bank* (Knox Report) (Abidjan: African Development Bank, 1994). On the effectiveness of aid more generally, the results of some of the more recent studies are conveniently summarized in the World Bank's publicly available version of its 1997 *Annual Review of Development Effectiveness* (Washington, D.C.: World Bank, November 24, 1997), 6–7.

6. World Bank, *Assessing Aid* (New York: Oxford University Press, 1998), 23.

7. Center for Strategic and International Studies (CSIS), Task Force on the Multilateral Development Banks, *The United States and the Multilateral Development Banks* (Washington, D.C.: CSIS, March 1998).

8. Ian Vasquez, "At the World Bank, Money Is No Object," *Wall Street Journal,* May 1, 1998, p. A15.

9. Jerome I. Levinson, "Statement before the Committee on Banking and Financial Services," November 13, 1997, p. 2.

10. "Bailing out Indonesia," *Financial Times,* November 3, 1997.

11. John Reed, "Europe Development Bank Gets a Black Eye in Russia," *Wall Street Journal,* September 10, 1998, p. A19.

12. They include Bruce Rich, *Mortgaging the Earth* (Boston: Beacon Press, 1994); Paul J. Nelson, *The World Bank and Non-Governmental Organizations* (New York: St. Martin's Press, 1995); and Catherine Caufield, *Masters of Illusion: The World Bank and the Poverty of Nations* (New York: Henry Holt, 1996).

13. Jay D. Hair et al., *Pangue Hydroelectric Project (Chile): An Independent Review of the International Finance Corporation's Compliance with Applicable World Bank Group Environmental and Social Requirements* (Washington, D.C.: World Bank, April 4, 1997), 35, 42–43.

14. Jonathan Sanford and Susan R. Fletcher, *Environmental Assessment and Information Policies in the Multilateral Development Banks: Impact of the Pelosi Amendment* (Washington, D.C.: Congressional Research Service, July 21, 1997), 29.

15. Lawyers Committee for Human Rights, *The World Bank, NGOs and Freedom of Association* (New York: Lawyers Committee for Human Rights, November 1997), 41–42.

16. Kay Treakle, "Accountability at the World Bank: What Does It Take?" Presentation for the 1998 meeting of the Latin American Studies Association, Chicago, Illinois, September 24–25, 1998, p. 20.

17. Shanti R. Conly and Joanne E. Epp, *Falling Short: The World Bank's Role in Population and Reproductive Health* (Washington, D.C.: Population Action International, 1997), viii, 32.

18. Jeffrey A. Winters, "Down with the World Bank," *Far Eastern Economic Review* (February 13, 1997): 29.

19. Marcus W. Brauchli, "Speak No Evil: Why the World Bank Failed to Anticipate Indonesia's Deep Crisis," *Wall Street Journal,* July 14, 1998, p. A1.

20. *Congressional Record,* November 13, 1997, S12530.

21. Nicholas Eberstadt, *Foreign Aid and American Purpose* (Washington, D.C.: American Enterprise Institute, 1988), 17–19.

22. Steven Kull, I. M. Destler, and Clay Ramsay, *The Foreign Policy Gap: How Policymakers Misread the Public* (College Park, Md.: University of Maryland, October 1997), 110.

23. David Gordon et al., *What Future for Aid?* (Washington, D.C.: Overseas Development Council and the Henry L. Stimson Center, November 1996), 18.

24. Miles Pomper, "Clinton Gains Last-Minute Victories on Foreign Policy Priorities," *Congressional Quarterly,* October 24, 1998, p. 2913.

25. U.S. House of Representatives, *Congressional Record,* October 19, 1998, p. H11103.

26. Bruce Rich, "The Smile on a Child's Face: From the Culture of Loan Approval to the Culture of Development Effectiveness?" (paper

presented at the Northwestern University Conference on Reinventing the World Bank, Evanston, Illinois, May 14–16, 1999), 22–23.

Notes to Chapter 2

1. Ian A. Bowles and Cyril F. Kormos, "Environmental Reform at the World Bank: The Role of the U.S. Congress," *Virginia Journal of International Law* 35, no. 4 (Summer 1995): 780–781.

2. Caufield, *Masters of Illusion*, 236.

3. Interviews by author with current and former U.S. Treasury officers, Washington, D.C., October 23, 1997, and January 7, 1998.

4. U.S. Department of the Treasury, *Shaping U.S. Participation in the International Financial Institutions* (Washington, D.C.: U.S. Department of the Treasury, February 1978), 127.

5. Senate Appropriations Committee Report for FY 1993, Senate Report No. 102–419, p. 76.

6. *Report of the Portfolio Management Task Force in the World Bank* (Wapenhans Report), *Report to the Task Force on Improving Project Quality in the Asian Development Bank* (Schultz Report), *Managing Effective Development in the Inter-American Development Bank* (Tapoma Report), *The Quest for Quality in the African Development Bank* (Knox Report).

7. Danish Ministry of Foreign Affairs, *Plan of Action*, 53.

8. Statement by Joseph Eichenberger, director of Treasury's Office of Multilateral Development Banks, Northwestern University Conference on Reinventing the World Bank, May 14–16, 1999.

9. At the time of author's interview with the directors of this office in the fall of 1997, the newest hire, to be the desk officer for the Asian Development Bank, had just been selected and given the junior-level grade of GS-9.

10. Examples include Ernest Stern, Ray Sternfeld, Hollis Chenery, and John Mellor.

11. Interview by author with Margaret Goodman, former staff consultant, House Committee on Foreign Affairs, Washington, D.C., November 10, 1997.

12. Confidential interview by author, Washington, D.C., February 18, 1998.

13. Currently AID has one individual working on this early warning list on a contract basis.

14. Sanford and Fletcher, "Executive Summary," in *Environmental Assessment*, 8.

15. Confidential interview by author, Washington, D.C., December 18, 1997.

16. Somewhat of an exception is the EPA officer who devotes full

time to MDB project review and, through expertise and NGO contacts, has carved out a more influential role, probably equal to Treasury's own environmental staff.

17. Based on author's periodic attendance at Tuesday Group meetings since their inception.

18. Author's impression from numerous conversations carried on with corporate representatives in the context of CSIS's project on U.S. interests in the multilateral development banks, 1995–1997.

19. The exception has long been the small concessional lending window in the Inter-American Development Bank where lack of U.S. support for a project prevents its approval.

20. Confidential interview by author with former U.S. official, Washington, D.C., October 22, 1997.

21. Richard W. Richardson and Jonas H. Haralz, *Moving to the Market: The World Bank in Transition* (Washington, D.C.: Overseas Development Council, 1995), 12–13.

22. Moises Naim, "The World Bank: Its Role, Governance, and Institutional Culture," in *Bretton Woods: Looking to the Future* (Washington, D.C.: Bretton Woods Commission, July 1994), 280.

23. Caufield, *Masters of Illusion*, 236.

24. Confidential interview by author, Washington, D.C., November 4, 1997.

25. Sanford and Fletcher, *Environmental Assessment*, 78.

26. Catherine Gwin, *U.S. Relations with the World Bank, 1945–1992* (Washington, D.C.: Brookings Institution, 1994), 82.

27. Sanford and Fletcher, *Environmental Assessment*, 90.

28. Interview by author with Barbara Bramble, vice president, National Wildlife Federation, Washington, D.C., December 10, 1997.

29. Confidential interview by author with former Treasury official, Washington, D.C., January 7, 1997.

30. Telephone interview by author with John Lopez, counsel, Subcommittee on Domestic and International Monetary Policy of the House Banking Committee, Washington, D.C., January 20, 1998.

31. Confidential joint interview by author with three former Treasury officers now in various MDBs, Washington, D.C., November 17, 1997.

32. Confidential interview by author with former Treasury Department official, Washington, D.C., October 21, 1997.

33. "An Asian Affair," *Financial Times*, May 6, 1999, p. 15; conversations with senior officials in several MDBs, Spring 1999; James Smalhout, "High-Wire Act That Changed the Bank," *Euromoney* (September 1999), 179.

34. Percy S. Mistry, *Multilateral Development Banks* (The Hague: Forum on Debt and Development, 1995), 256.

35. William Ryrie, *First World, Third World* (New York: St. Martin's Press, 1995), 163–164.

36. Anne O. Krueger, *Economic Policies at Cross-Purposes* (Washington, D.C.: Brookings Institution, 1993), 100–101.

37. Paul Blustein, "World Bank's Role Evolves with Crisis," *Washington Post*, September 25, 1998, p. F2.

38. Diana Tussie, *The Inter-American Development Bank* (Boulder, Colorado: Lynne Rienner Publishers, 1995), 139.

39. Confidential interviews by author, Washington, D.C., December 17, 1998.

40. Nihal Kappagoda, *The Asian Development Bank* (Boulder, Colorado: Lynne Rienner Publishers, 1995), 33; and Dennis T. Yasutomo, *The New Multilateralism in Japan's Foreign Policy* (New York: St. Martin's Press, 1995), 100.

41. L. Ronald Scheman, "Banking on Growth: The Role of the Inter-American Development Bank," *Journal of Interamerican Studies and World Affairs* 39, no. 1 (Spring 1997): 98.

42. Interview by author with Thomas Duesterberg, former assistant secretary for international economic policy, Department of Commerce, Washington, D.C., December 5, 1997.

43. Curt Tarnoff and Larry Q. Nowels, *U.S. Foreign Assistance: The Rationale, the Record, and the Challenges in the Post–Cold War Era* (Washington, D.C.: National Planning Association, 1994), 23.

44. Interview by author with Jerome I. Levinson, Washington, D.C., December 11, 1997.

45. Gwin, *U.S. Relations with the World Bank, 1945–1992,* p. 83.

46. Interview by author with Arnold Nachmanoff, Washington, D.C., November 5, 1997, and with James W. Conrow, Fairfax, Virginia, October 21, 1997.

47. The portfolio review for the World Bank found that "the number of projects judged unsatisfactory at completion increased from 15 percent of the cohort reviewed in FY81 to . . . 37.5 percent of the FY91 cohort." *Report of the Portfolio Management Task Force,* ii.

48. Confidential interview by author, Washington, D.C., November 5, 1997.

49. Some criticism can be found in Gwin, *U.S. Relations with the World Bank, 1945–1992,* pp. 83–84; and Ryrie, *First World, Third World,* 175.

50. Interview by author with Tim Rieser, staff, Foreign Operations Subcommittee of the Senate Committee on Appropriations, Washington, D.C., December 12, 1997.

51. The case of the executive vice president of the IDB whose tenure was abruptly ended early in the Reagan administration was an irritant for years with key figures in Congress.

52. This section is based on the author's notes from this period including meetings where a number of foreign officials discussed this matter.

53. Yasutomo, *The New Multilateralism,* 98.

54. This occurred in the case of several ADB jobs in the 1980s.

55. U.S. Congress, *Legislation on Foreign Relations through 1994* (Washington, D.C.: U.S. Government Printing Office, May 1995), 135–136.

56. Interview by author with Jonathan Sanford, former staff director, House Banking Subcommittee on Domestic and International Monetary Policy, Washington, D.C., August 6, 1997.

57. Nelson, *The World Bank and Non-Governmental Organizations,* 103–105.

58. Jerome I. Levinson, "Statement before the Committee on Banking and Financial Services Concerning East Asian Economic Conditions," November 13, 1997.

59. Bowles and Kormos, "Environmental Reform at the World Bank," 829–830.

60. Examples made available to the CSIS task force on the United States and MDBs, in many cases by NGOs, are listed in appendix D of CSIS, *The United States and the Multilateral Development Banks,* 108–112.

61. Helen Dewar, "Senate Panel Ties Strings to $18 Billion for IMF," *Washington Post,* March 18, 1998, A5.

62. Gwin, *U.S. Relations with the World Bank, 1945–1992,* pp. 76, 84.

Notes to Chapter 3

1. Confidential interview by author, Washington, D.C., November 5, 1997.

2. James B. Burnham, "Understanding the World Bank: A Dispassionate Analysis," in *Perpetuating Poverty: The World Bank, the IMF, and the Developing World,* ed. Doug Bandow and Ian Vasquez (Washington, D.C.: Cato Institute, 1994), 84–85.

3. Nelson, *The World Bank and Non-Governmental Organizations,* 125.

4. World Bank, *The Strategic Compact,* 4.

5. Naim, "The World Bank: Its Role, Governance and Organizational Culture," 282.

6. Mistry, *Multilateral Development Banks,* 257.

7. Interview by author with C. Patrick Coady, former U.S. executive director at the World Bank, Washington, D.C., December 3, 1997, and with Larry K. Mellinger, former U.S. executive director at the Inter-American Development Bank, Washington, D.C., December 5, 1997.

8. Paul Blustein, "Missionary Work," *Washington Post Magazine,* November 10, 1996, 11.

9. Some of the most recent outside studies are quoted in chapter 1. Some of the disturbing MDB evaluation data is summarized in the CSIS task force report, *The United States and the Multilateral Development Banks,*

46, 64–65, 108–112, and in U.S. Government Accounting Office (GAO) Report, *World Bank: U.S. Interests Supported but Oversight Needed to Help Ensure Improved Performance* (Washington, D.C.: GAO, September 1996), 42–43.

10. U.S. Agency for International Development, *Development and the National Interest: U.S. Economic Assistance into the 21st Century* (Washington, D.C.: U.S. Agency for International Development, February 1989), 10.

11. Diana Tussie, *The Inter-American Development Bank* (Boulder, Colorado: Lynne Rienner, Publishers, 1995), 31. Also Kapur, Lewis, and Webb, *The World Bank: Its First Half Century,* vol. 1, pp. 3, 676. This perception also was confirmed in various interviews by author.

12. Even the smallest and poorest countries have some votes in the MDBs to emphasize their participation in institutional governance, but their relative share is usually small in comparison to those of the large donor countries.

13. In most cases MDB voting rights are related to hard window contributions. Nonetheless, real influence is related to total financial support for the institution.

14. This section is based on notes from author's participation in this long series of negotiations, 1985–1989.

15. In 1981 the incoming Reagan administration conducted an extensive analysis of the MDBs as a group and made decisions about how it saw them fitting into its overall foreign economic policies. The results are contained in U.S. Department of the Treasury, *United States Participation in the Multilateral Development Banks in the 1980s,* Washington, D.C., February 1982.

16. Congressman Lee Hamilton, "Remarks on the Activity of the Foreign Affairs Committee Task Force on Foreign Assistance" (remarks delivered at meeting of the Board for International Food and Agricultural Development, Washington, D.C., September 14, 1988), 7–8.

17. Julia Chang Bloch, "Can Foreign Aid Contribute to U.S. Leadership Abroad?" in *Foreign Assistance in a Time of Constraints,* ed. Richard S. Belous, S. Dahlia Stein, and Nita Christine Kent (Washington, D.C.; National Planning Association, 1995), 17.

18. Krueger, *Economic Policies at Cross-Purposes,* 63.

19. President's Commission on the Management of AID Programs, *Critical Underlying Issues—Further Analysis* (Washington, D.C., December 22, 1992), 3, 50.

20. Interview by author with Michael O'Hanlon, Brookings Institution, Washington, D.C., December 9, 1997.

21. Tarnoff and Nowels, *U.S. Foreign Asistance,* 9.

22. World Bank, *Assessing Aid,* 5.

23. Ryrie, *First World, Third World,* 48–49.

24. Commission on Security and Economic Assistance (Carlucci

Commission), *A Report to the Secretary of State* (Washington, D.C., 1983), 4, 50.

25. President's Commission on the Management of AID Programs, *Critical Underlying Issues*, 51.

26. Exceptions are the cases where UN agencies consider documents on global financial issues, such as debt, where Treasury provides guidance to the State Department on a U.S. position.

27. Commission on Security and Economic Assistance, *A Report to the Secretary of State*, 52.

28. L. Ronald Scheman, "Banking on Growth," 98–99.

29. Commission on Security and Economic Assistance, A *Report to the Secretary of State*, 53.

30. Interview by author with Reuben Sternfeld, former executive vice president, Inter-American Development Bank, Washington, D.C., October 22, 1997.

31. Confidential interview by author, Washington, D.C., November 17, 1997.

32. This was the congressional appropriation for "USAID-managed programs" in FY 1999. Curt Tarnoff and Larry Nowels, *Foreign Aid: An Introductory Overview of U.S. Programs and Policy* (Washington, D.C.: Congressional Research Service, November 6, 1998), 18.

33. Among others, former congressman Matt McHugh, currently counselor to the president of the World Bank, thought that when there are significant issues about the MDBs, confining discussions to a small group may well not work, and although broadening the group of members consulted could be risky from the executive branch's perspective, in the end it is a sounder approach. Interview by author with Matt McHugh, Washington, D.C., November 4, 1997.

34. Confidential interview by author, Washington, D.C., October 28, 1997.

35. Devesh Kapur, remarks at the Northwestern University Conference on Reinventing the World Bank, Evanston, Illinois, May 14–16, 1999.

36. Confidential telephone interview by author with a senior World Bank official, Washington, D.C., June 2, 1999.

37. Yasutomo, *The New Multilateralism*, 81.

Notes to Chapter 4

1. President's Special Review Board, *The Tower Commission Report* (New York: Bantam Books, Times Books, 1987), V-2.

2. The strategy called for here would be much more specific than the short document produced by the Treasury Department covering all

of its international programs called "Strategic Plan for Treasury International Programs." This document, produced in response to the requirements of the Government Performance and Results Act, is so general and full of unspecific hortatory statements that it is impossible to ascertain U.S. priorities.

3. Such an "all spigots review" was suggested by John Bolton, former State Department assistant secretary for international organization affairs and former head of policy for USAID, in an interview with the author, Washington, D.C., December 15, 1997.

4. Confidential interview by author with representative of a major MDB shareholder government, Washington, D.C., October 24, 1997.

5. Interview by author with Matt McHugh, former congressman and counselor to the World Bank president, Washington, D.C., November 4, 1997.

6. Interview by author with Susan B. Levine, former Treasury deputy assistant secretary for international development, debt, and environment policy, Washington, D.C., December 12, 1997.

7. Commission on Security and Economic Assistance, *A Report to the Secretary of State*, 54.

8. I. M. Destler, *The National Economic Council: A Work in Progress* (Washington, D.C.: Institute for International Economics, November 1996), 11.

9. Memorandum from Congressman Lee Hamilton to Deputy Secretary of State Clifton Wharton, April 29, 1993, p. 2.

10. President's Commission on the Management of AID Programs, *Critical Underlying Issues*, 53–54.

11. President's Special Review Board, *The Tower Commission Report*, V-3-4, and Destler, *The National Economic Council*, 38–39.

12. Destler, *The National Economic Council*, 26, 29, 36.

13. Interview by author with James D. Bond and Richard Collins, former staff directors of the Senate Appropriations Subcommittee on Foreign Operations, Arlington, Virginia, November 3, 1997.

14. The exception would be the IMF, which is often considered more of a short-term financial stabilization and regulatory entity than an agency making long-term transfers. Under this option, U.S. participation in the IMF would continue to be overseen by the Treasury Department.

15. Jeffrey E. Garten, "Lessons for the Next Financial Crisis," *Foreign Affairs* 78, no. 2 (March/April 1999): 91.

16. President's Commission on the Management of AID Programs, *Critical Underlying Issues*, 44. One of the most comprehensive visions of a changed State Department focusing on cross-cutting issues was provided by Richard Collins and James D. Bond, former staff directors of the Subcommittee on Foreign Operations, Senate Appropriations Committee, interview by author, Arlington, Va., November 3, 1997.

17. Interview by author with John Bolton, former assistant secretary of state for international organization affairs, Washington, D.C., December 15, 1997. The need for stronger specialized expertise and for policies to reward such expertise on the part of State Department officers was also recommended recently in Center for Strategic and International Studies (CSIS), *Reinventing Diplomacy in the Information Age* (Washington, D.C.: CSIS, October 9, 1998), 38; and in Henry L. Stimson Center, *Equipped for the Future: Managing U.S. Foreign Affairs in the 21st Century* (Washington, D.C.: Stimson Center, October 1998), 13.

18. Jeffrey E. Garten, "Business and Foreign Policy," *Foreign Affairs* 76, no. 3 (May/June 1997): 69.

19. A recent article especially notes the problem with respect to trade policy. "Tragically, Washington remains ill equipped to tackle the protectionist challenge head-on. Trade policy-making has traditionally rested in the executive branch of the government with the USTR—a small and relatively weak office. Its bureaucracy is fragmented: although the USTR negotiates trade agreements, he or she plays no role in implementing them or in handling the adjustment costs that arise, which other departments cover." Marcus Noland, "Learning to Love the WTO," *Foreign Affairs* 78, no. 5 (September-October 1999): 90.

20. "Overseas Aid: Stop Short," *Economist,* August 16, 1997, p. 45.

21. Among others, a Council on Foreign Relations task force recently recommended that the World Bank "should not be involved in crisis lending or crisis management." *Safeguarding Prosperity in a Global Financial System,* Report of an Independent Task Force Sponsored by the Council on Foreign Relations (Washington, D.C.: Institute for International Economics, September 1999).

22. World Bank, *Annual Review of Development Effectiveness* (Washington, D.C.: World Bank, November 24, 1997), 3.

23. Jonathan Fox, associate professor of social sciences, University of California, Santa Cruz, "The World Bank Inspection Panel: Lessons from the First Four Years" (paper presented at the Northwestern University Conference on Reinventing the World Bank, Evanston, Illinois, May 14–16, 1999), 18. More detailed analysis of the World Bank's compliance with its policies can be found in Jonathan Fox and L. David Brown, *The Struggle for Accountability* (Cambridge, Mass.: MIT Press, 1998), 515–527. A very recent example of the problem is given in a *Financial Times* article of September 24, 1999, which quotes a new internal World Bank study that found "a disconnect between Bank policy and practice" in considering the impact of structural and sectoral loans on the poor and the environment. Nancy Dunne, "World Bank Failed on Environment and the Poor," *Financial Times,* September 24, 1999, p. 10.

24. Jane Loos, "Options to Reduce Negative impact from Corruption

on Bank-Financed Activities," World Bank memorandum, October 19, 1998, p. 2.

25. A more thorough discussion of the type of information on project status that is needed can be found in the report of the CSIS Task Force on the Multilateral Development Banks, *The United States and the Multilateral Development Banks,* 70–79.

26. Interview by author with Lionel C. Johnson, vice president, international government relations, Citicorp, and former Treasury deputy assistant secretary for international development, debt, and environment policy, Washington, D.C., January 7, 1998.

27. Center for Strategic and International Studies, *Reinventing Diplomacy,* 10, 50; and Stimson Center, *Equipped for the Future,* 6–7.

28. Interview by author with Phyllis Shearer Jones, former assistant U.S. special trade representative for intergovernmental affairs and public liaison, Washington, D.C., December 16, 1997.

29. Ibid.

30. Ibid.

31. Committee to Review the Australian Overseas Aid Program, *One Clear Objective: Poverty Reduction through Sustainable Development* (Canberra: AusAID, April 1997), v, 331–337.

32. The suggestion for more intense capital-to-capital consultations was made particularly by the U.S. executive director at the ADB, Linda Tsao-Yang, on the basis of her experience in that bank in comments at Northwestern University's Conference on Reinventing the World Bank, Evanston, Illinois, May 14–16, 1999.

33. Deepak Gopinath makes the case in a recent article that the Treasury Department has eroded much of the States Department's role on most foreign economic issues, often with what seems likely to be negative consequences for long-term U.S. policy. Deepak Gopinath, "Who's the Boss?" *Institutional Investor* (September 1999), 90–94.

34. David Wessel and Bob Davis, "How Global Crisis Grew Despite Efforts of a Crack U.S. Team," *Wall Street Journal,* September 24, 1998, p. A1.

35. Kevin Muehring, "The Fire Next Time," *Institutional Investor* (September 1998), 94. The same point is made in James Smalhout's "Seven-Point Plan to Save the World," *Euromoney* (September 1999), 187.

36. Garten, "Lessons for the Next Financial Crisis," 90.

37. Michael M. Phillips, "World Bank Board Agrees to Weaken a Watchdog Panel," *Wall Street Journal,* April 21, 1999, p. A6.

38. James Burnham, "The IMF and the World Bank: Time to Merge," *Washington Quarterly* 22, no. 2 (Spring 1999): 109.

39. These issues are discussed in, among others, Robert Chote, "World Bank Sounds Alarm over Risky Emergency Loans," *Financial Times,* September 25, 1998, and Tony Tassell, "After the 'Miracle,' ADB

Debates Its Future Role," *Financial Times,* December 22, 1998. The independent task force on international financial architecture sponsored by the Council on Foreign Relations recently concluded that the World Bank should not be involved in such crisis lending (see "Safeguarding Prosperity," 19, 116).

40. Congressman Jim Leach, "Opening Statement," in House Committee on Banking and Financial Services, *Hearing on Proposals for a New International Financial Architecture,* May 20, 1999, p. 2.

Notes to Chapter 5

1. Author's interview with William Marsh, former U.S. permanent representative to the UN Agencies in Rome and Geneva, Washington, D.C., October 27, 1997.

2. Natsios, *U.S. Foreign Policy and the Four Horsemen of the Apocalypse,* 82.

3. Gary Ostrower, *The United Nations and the United States* (New York: Simon and Schuster Macmillan, 1998), 231.

4. Author's interview with William Marsh.

5. Danish Ministry of Foreign Affairs, *Plan of Action for Active Multilateralism,* 44.

6. Stefan Halper, the author of a number of publications on the UN system, believes the inconsistency of the approaches taken by sequential State Department assistant secretaries in charge of the UN was one of the reasons that the United States did not make greater headway in its efforts to deal with UN management weaknesses. "The UN never felt that there was a consistent and coherent U.S. focus on management reform." Author's telephone interview with Stefan Halper, Washington, D.C., February 25, 1998. This factor also was noted in Ostrower, *The United Nations,* 233.

7. Edward Luck, "Reforming the United Nations," in *Delusions of Grandeur: The United Nations and Global Intervention,* ed. Ted Galen Carpenter (Washington, D.C.: Cato Institute, 1997), 154–155.

8. Krueger, *Economic Policies at Cross-Purposes,* 182.

9. Author's confidential interview with senior UN official, Washington, D.C., January 13, 1998.

10. John M. Goshko, "U.S. Will Fight to Keep Top UN Development Post," *Washington Post,* September 9, 1998, p. A23. Stefan Halper notes that the individual in this position had been replaced 7 times in 8 years before mid-1994 when a former Price Waterhouse executive took over. Previously, the job had been held "mostly by political appointees, many of whom were inherently disinterested in management." Stefan Halper,

A Miasma of Corruption: The United Nations at 50 (Washington, D.C.: Cato Institute, April 30, 1996), 11.

11. The Nordic countries, among others, have been unhappy about the strong U.S. pressure exerted to secure the selection of U.S. candidates to head three of the UN aid agencies at a time when the Nordic countries' financial contributions to two of the three entities exceeded those of the United States.

12. Author's interview with William Marsh.

13. As quoted in E. J. Dionne, Jr., "Globalism with a Human Face," *Washington Post*, May 29, 1998, A27.

14. Devesh Kapur, "The IMF: A Cure or a Curse?" *Foreign Policy*, no. 111 (Summer 1998): 128.

Select Bibliography

Books

Bandow, Doug, and Ian Vasquez, ed. *Perpetuating Poverty: The World Bank, the IMF, and the Developing World.* Washington, D.C.: Cato Institute, 1994.

Bretton Woods Commission. *Bretton Woods: Looking to the Future.* Washington, D.C., 1994.

Carpenter, Ted, ed. *Delusions of Grandeur: The United Nations and Global Intervention.* Washington, D.C.: Cato Institute, 1997.

Caufield, Catherine. *Masters of Illusion: The World Bank and the Poverty of Nations.* New York: Henry Holt and Company, 1996.

Center for Strategic and International Studies (CSIS). *Reinventing Diplomacy in the Information Age.* Washington, D.C.: CSIS, October 9, 1998.

______. Task Force on the Multilateral Development Banks. *The United States and the Multilateral Development Banks.* Washington, D.C.: CSIS, 1998.

Commission on Security and Economic Assistance (Carlucci Commission). *A Report to the Secretary of State.* Washington, D.C., 1983.

Committee to Review the Australian Overseas Aid Program. *One Clear Objective: Poverty Reduction through Sustainable Development.* Canberra: AusAID, 1997.

Conly, Shanti R., and Joanne E. Epp. *Falling Short: The World Bank's Role in Population and Reproductive Health.* Washington, D.C.: Population Action International, 1997.

Council on Foreign Relations. Independent Task Force on the Future International Financial Architecture. *Safeguarding Prosperity in a Global Financial System.* Washington, D.C.: Institute for International Economics, 1999.

Culpeper, Roy. *Canada and the Global Governors.* Ottawa: North-South Institute, 1994.

———. *The Multilateral Development Banks: Titans or Behemoths?* Boulder, Colorado: Lynne Rienner Publishers, 1997.

Culpeper, Roy, and Andrew Clark. *High Stakes and Low Incomes: Canada and the Multilateral Development Banks.* Ottawa: North-South Institute, 1994.

Danish Ministry of Foreign Affairs. *Effectiveness of Multilateral Agencies at Country Level.* Copenhagen, 1991.

———. *Plan of Action for Active Multilateralism.* Copenhagen, 1996.

Destler, I.M. *The National Economic Council: A Work in Progress.* Washington, D.C.: Institute for International Economics, 1996.

Eberstadt, Nicholas. *Foreign Aid and American Purpose.* Washington, D.C.: American Enterprise Institute, 1988.

Eichengreen, Barry. *Toward a New International Financial Architecture.* Washington, D.C.: Institute for International Economics, 1999.

English, E. Philip, and Harris M. Mule. *The African Development Bank.* Boulder, Colorado: Lynne Rienner Publishers, 1996.

Fox, Jonathan A., and L. David Brown, ed. *The Struggle for Accountability: The World Bank, NGOs, and Grassroots Movements.* Cambridge, Massachusetts: MIT Press, 1998.

Gwin, Catherine. *U.S. Relations with the World Bank, 1945-1992.* Washington, D.C.: Brookings Institution, 1994.

Henry L. Stimson Center. *Equipped for the Future: Managing U.S. Foreign Affairs in the 21st Century.* Washington, D.C.: Stimson Center, October 1998.

Kappagoda, Nihal. *The Asian Development Bank.* Boulder, Colorado: Lynne Rienner Publishers, 1995.

Kapur, Devesh, John P. Lewis, and Richard Webb. *The World Bank: Its First Half Century.* Vols. 1 and 2. Washington, D.C.: Brookings Institution, 1997.

Karns, Margaret P., and Karen A. Mingst, ed. *The United States and Multilateral Institutions.* London: Routledge, 1992.

Krueger, Anne O. *Economic Policies at Cross-Purposes.* Washington, D.C.: Brookings Institution, 1993.

Kull, Steven, I.M. Destler, and Clay Ramsey. *The Foreign Policy Gap: How Policymakers Misread the Public.* College Park, Maryland: University of Maryland, 1997.

Mistry, Percy S. *Multilateral Development Banks.* The Hague: Forum on Debt and Development, 1995.

Natsios, Andrew. *U.S. Foreign Policy and the Four Horsemen of the Apocalypse.* Westport, Conn.: Praeger/CSIS, 1997.

Nelson, Paul J. *The World Bank and Non-Governmental Organizations.* New York: St. Martin's Press, 1995.

O'Hanlon, Michael, and Carol Graham. *A Half Penny on the Federal Dollar: The Future of Development Aid.* Washington, D.C.: Brookings Institution, 1997.

Ostrower, Gary B. *The United Nations and the United States.* New York: Simon and Schuster Macmillan, 1998.

Polak, Jacques J. *The World Bank and the IMF.* Washington, D.C.: Brookings Institution, 1994.

President's Commission on the Management of AID Programs. *Critical Underlying Issues—Further Analysis.* Washington, D.C., 1992.

Rich, Bruce. *Mortgaging the Earth: The World Bank, Environmental Impoverishment, and the Crisis of Development.* Boston: Beacon Press, 1994.

Richardson, Richard W., and Jonas H. Haralz. *Moving to the Market: The World Bank in Transition.* Washington, D.C.: Overseas Development Council, 1995.

Ryrie, William. *First World, Third World.* New York: St. Martin's Press, 1995.

Sanford, Jonathan E. *U.S. Foreign Policy and Multilateral Development Banks.* Boulder, Colorado: Westview Press, 1982.

Sanford, Jonathan, and Susan R. Fletcher. *Environmental Assessment and Information Policies in the Multilateral Development Banks.* Washington, D.C.: Congressional Research Service, July 21, 1997.

Tarnoff, Curt, and Larry Q. Nowels. *U.S. Foreign Assistance: The Rationale, the Record, and the Challenges in the Post–Cold War Era.* Washington, D.C.: National Planning Association, 1994.

Tussie, Diana. *The Inter-American Development Bank.* Boulder, Colorado: Lynne Rienner Publishers, 1995.

U.S. Department of the Treasury. *United States Participation in the Multilateral Development Banks in the 1980s.* Washington, D.C.: U.S. Department of the Treasury, 1982.

U.S. General Accounting Office (GAO). *World Bank: U.S. Interests Supported, but Oversight Needed to Help Ensure Improved Performance.* Washington, D.C.: GAO, September 1996. NOTE: Author also reviewed other GAO reports, too numerous to cite here, concerning U.S. participation in various multilateral organizations.

World Bank. *Annual Review of Development Effectiveness.* Washington, D.C.: World Bank, November 24, 1997.

______. *Assessing Aid.* New York: Oxford University Press, 1998.

Yasutomo, Dennis T. *The New Multilateralism in Japan's Foreign Policy.* New York: St. Martin's Press, 1995.

Articles

Bowles, Ian A., and Cyril F. Kormos. "Environmental Reform at the World Bank: The Role of the U.S. Congress." *Virginia Journal of International Law* 35, no. 4 (Summer 1995).

Burnham, James B. "The IMF and the World Bank: Time to Merge." *Washington Quarterly* 22, no. 2 (Spring 1999).

Eagleburger, Lawrence S., and Robert L. Barry. "Dollars and Sense Diplomacy: A Better Foreign Policy for Less Money." *Foreign Affairs* 75, no. 4 (July/August 1996).

Garten, Jeffrey E. "Lessons for the Next Financial Crisis." *Foreign Affairs* 78, no. 2 (March/April 1999).

———. "Business and Foreign Policy." *Foreign Affairs* 76, no. 3 (May/June 1997).

Gopinath, Deepak. "Who's the Boss?" *Institutional Investor* (September 1999).

Haass, Richard N., and Robert E. Litan. "Globalization and Its Discontents." *Foreign Affairs* 77, no. 3 (May/June 1998).

Kapur, Devesh. "The IMF: A Cure or a Curse?" *Foreign Policy*, no. 111 (Summer 1998).

Krueger, Anne. "Whither the World Bank and the IMF?" Working Paper No. 23, Center for Research on Economic Development and Policy Reform, Stanford University (August 1998).

Muehring, Kevin. "The Fire Next Time." *Institutional Investor* (September 1998).

Noland, Marcus. "Learning to Love the WTO." *Foreign Affairs* 78, no. 5 (September/October 1999).

"Pope Kofi's Unruly Flock." *Economist*. August 8, 1998.

Sanford, Jonathan, and Margaret Goodman. "Congressional Oversight and the Multilateral Development Banks." *International Organization* 29, no. 4 (Autumn 1975).

Scheman, L. Ronald. "Banking on Growth: The Role of the Inter-American Development Bank." *Journal of Interamerican Studies and World Affairs* 39, no. 1 (Spring 1997).

Smalhout, James. "High-Wire Act That Changed the Bank," *Euromoney* (September 1999).

———. "Seven-Point Plan to Save the World," *Euromoney* (September 1999).

Treakle, Kay. "Accountability at the World Bank: What Does It Take?" Presentation for the 1998 meeting of the Latin American Studies Association. Chicago, Illinois, September 24–25, 1998.

Winters, Jeffrey A. "Down with the World Bank." *Far Eastern Economic Review* (February 13, 1997).

Index

About the Author

Barbara Upton was director of the Center for Strategic and International Studies project on the United States and the Multilateral Development Banks (MDBs). In the first phase of the project, a task force chaired by former senator Bill Bradley and Congressman John Kasich produced recommendations for future U.S. policy toward the MDBs. The report of the task force, published by CSIS in 1998, was endorsed by seven additional members of Congress and a number of business leaders, former senior government officials, academic experts, and leaders of nongovernmental organizations.

Ms. Upton is a Phi Beta Kappa graduate of the Georgetown University School of Foreign Service and received a master's degree from the Fletcher School of Law and Diplomacy. She directed the U.S. Agency for International Development's liaison with the MDBs, UN aid agencies, and other official aid donors for a number of years, and earlier she served as a finance officer for Latin America and the Caribbean. While a U.S. governmental official, she participated in U.S. negotiating teams for all MDB funding negotiations from 1981 until 1995. Currently Ms. Upton is engaged in private sector business activities.

ISBN 0-275-96966-5

90000>

EAN

9 780275 969660

HARDCOVER BAR CODE